Media Manifestos

V

Media Manifestos

On the Technological Transmission of Cultural Forms

RÉGIS DEBRAY

Translated by
Eric Rauth

VERSO
London • New York

First published by Verso 1996
This edition © Verso 1996
Translation © Eric Rauth 1996
First published as *Manifestes médialogiques*
© Éditions Gallimard 1994
All rights reserved

The right of Eric Rauth to be identified as the translator
of this work has been asserted by him in accordance with
the Copyright, Designs and Patents Act 1988

Verso
UK: 6 Meard Street, London W1V 3HR
USA: 180 Varick Street, New York NY 10014–4606

Verso is the imprint of New Left Books

ISBN 1–85984–972–5
ISBN 1–85984–087–6 (pbk)

British Library Cataloguing in Publication Data
A catalogue record for this book is available from the British Library

Library of Congress Cataloging-in-Publication Data
Debray, Régis.
  [Manifestes médialogiques. English]
  Media manifestos : on the technological transmission of
cultural forms / Régis Debray : translated by Eric Rauth.
      p.   cm.
  Text submitted as part of the viva, or dissertation defense,
confirming the candidate's authority to direct research. Presented
at the Sorbonne (Paris I) on Jan. 8, 1994
  Includes bibliographical references.
  ISBN 1–85984–972–5. — ISBN 1–85984–087–6 (pbk.)
  1. Mass media—Philosophy.   2. Semiotics.   3. Philosophy,
French—20th century.   4. Mass media and technology.   I. Title.
P90.D4313 1996
302.23′01—dc20   95–51442
                                                        CIP

Typeset by M Rules
Printed and bound in Great Britain by Biddles Ltd,
Guildford and King's Lynn

This book has been published with the financial assistance of
the French Ministry of Culture

Behold a canvas vast.
Set upon it golden arabesques.

Victor Hugo

Contents

PART ONE

FOR A MEDIOLOGY

A Note about Context

This text was submitted as part of the viva or dissertation defense confirming the candidate's authority to direct research. It was presented at the Sorbonne (Paris I) on January 8, 1994, to a committee composed of Messrs. Daniel Bougnoux, Bernard Bourgeois (presiding), Roger Chartier, François Dagognet (minutes), Jacques Le Goff and Michel Serres.

I

Identity Card

"Mediology" may seem an ambiguous and even dubious term. Its meaning needs to be distilled. Before doing so I want briefly to retrace the steps that have led to this disciplinary project.

1. Reminder

They have taken some twists and turns, beginning with the contemporary mediator represented by the modern French intellectual (*Teachers, Writers, Celebrities*, 1979; *The Scribe*, 1980), ascending to *mediation* per se in its ageless logical necessity (*Critique of Political Reason*, 1983), only to arrive finally at the *media* or the contemporary procedures of influence (*Courses in General Mediology*, 1991; *A History of the Western Eye*, 1992; *The Seducer State*, 1993).*

At the outset, I was concerned with probing the too familiar term *ideology*. It had appeared to me, despite the Marxist legacy, that "ideology" would only become clearer when removed from the semantic field of the *epistemè* to that of *praxis*; the misleading notion of ideology as *the antithesis of scientific knowledge* leads to our understanding it as illusion or mere reflection, a

*Chapter VIII of *A History of the Western Eye* appears as "The Three Ages of Looking" in *Critical Inquiry* 21 (Spring 1995), pp. 529–55. Chapter II is published in *Common Knowledge*, vol. 4, no. 2 (Fall 1995) under the title "The Image v. Language: Transmitting Symbols." [Trs.]

specular inversion of the real, lack of true recognition, false consciousness, etc. It is better to think of it as the means *of a form of organization*. Of an incorporation. Of a collective incarnation. Questions that were once said to be ideological we would today say are symbolic or cultural. They torment and beset the body politic, which is why they are neither trifling nor hazy questions, but weighty, serious and "organic." In this perspective and sticking with cliches, religion is no longer the opium of the people but the vitamin pills of the feeble.

It appeared clear to me following this that these practices of organization were, throughout history, grouped along a recurrent axis, which was fortunately variable in its forms but unfortunately stable in its principle: the axiom of incompleteness, where to my eyes the religious syntax of collective life is established/born.

I sum up this logical mechanism inspired by Gödel: no general totality of relations is relative to itself or it would not then be a totality. A system cannot close itself off by making sole use of the elements internal to it. The closing off of a field can thus only proceed contradictorily, by opening up to an element external to this same field. This element will turn out to be a founding hero, an originary myth, Holy Scripture, a Constitution or Testament—will always be what is sacred to a given group, what it lost in the beginning and what it must incessantly offer itself anew, symbolically, in order to reconstitute itself as a group.

If the structural invariant of stable societies is indeed like this, there will always be among us a near nothing, some ungraspable and inexhaustible je-ne-sais-quoi to transmit. Since no geographical territory can be completely closed off horizontally, the god-making machinery stops only where human communities are marked off and effectively exist, and mediation's work is endless. Even the smallest organized group will have need of a body of mediators or intellectuals [*clercs*] to periodically re-bestow coherence and vigor by opening it to a supereminent value.

Here I will mention that work of mine of religious anthropology (*Critique of Political Reason*). Even though [since it is more a work concerned with the political forms of the sacred] it does not belong to the mediological edifice, it ensures its foundations, at least to my way of thinking. The ever-renewed organs of the *inter-* are spurred on back upstream by the *meta-* function. It is the transcendence of the Origin, founded by logic, which brings it about that interpreters exist. Within a pure immanence no messengers are needed. Our religions have recourse to angels because God isn't there.

Once the *why* (why there is something symbolic in circulation) was elucidated, if I may be so bold, there remained the *how* (how an abstract symbol can produce concrete effects). This *how* was an avowed constant that went under the name of "symbolic efficacy." It called for a more specific conceptual apparatus which I called "mediology" in the first line of *Teachers, Writers, Celebrities* back in 1979.

There is then a thesis at stake here. What at bottom is its argument?

It comes down to replacing one word with another: "communication" with "mediation." Perhaps you will say that this is a rather paltry result of fifteen years' labor. But passing from a philosophy of communication to a philosophy of mediation is to change elements. "The Mediator supplants the messenger": isn't this the very formula of the Christian revolution? The rubble of Mercury's statue strewn before Christ on the cross. It was Michel Serres who led me to discover, in Raphael's Vatican Stanze, that fresco by Lauretti Tommaso christened *The Triumph of Christianity*. It was in that case truly a triumph over Hermes. The Word cannot transmit itself without becoming Flesh, and the Flesh cannot be all love and glory; it is blood, sweat and tears. Transmission is never seraphic because incarnate. Christ has no wings to fly away from the cross, and the bodies of those Word-messengers the Angels are too tenuous and fine-spun to suit the purpose. The act of communication is fluid; that of mediation, weighty. The messenger-angel traverses space by flying through and above it, the mediator is *traversed by* time and transfixed by the centurion's lance. Rational mediology too, taking the founding Christian myth as paradigm, is tragic twice over: because it takes the trouble to say what suffering, misery and exclusion are inscribed in any effective transmission of a message, and because it works on the obstacle or perverse effect of the systems of delivery [*messageries*], namely that the good messenger is he who disappears behind his message like the angel of the Annunciation, vanishing as soon as it appears. But in historical practice, it is the mediator who outpaces what he mediates, and the connecting conduit also blocks alternate routes (Saint Paul/Christ, Lenin/Marx, Lacan/Freud, etc.). The intermediary makes the law. Mediation determines the nature of the message, relation has primacy over being. To put it in other terms, it is bodies that think and not minds. The constraint of incorporation produces the corporations—those intermediate bodies and institutions of knowledge, normatized and normative, which we call schools, churches, parties, associations, societies of thinkers, etc.

2. Identity Check

If, in the course of some hypothetical spot-check, this rather suspicious-looking neologism of mediology were obliged to state its identity (the way a Parisian can be asked to present his papers in the metro), the question about its line of work could be answered, "I deal not so much with forms of mass media per se, despite the name I wear. My business is really signs."

"Linguistics has been handling that one for quite some time," the border policeman would retort. "To be sure, but I understand 'sign' in the wider sense, and not just as it has been endowed with traits recognized by linguists—the arbitrary, the differential, the linear, the discrete. I handle all the sensory traces of an intended meaning." "But that is semiology's bailiwick."

"Others are indeed concerned with the *meaning of signs*. I'm interested in the *power of signs*—an altogether different problem."

"Which the pragmatists of communication for the Palo Alto school at Stanford have undertaken to formulate."

"Undoubtedly, yet the Palo Alto school and the specialists of language or speech acts concentrate on what is produced in *verbal* communication, between two or several interlocutors. I have in view, beyond-word relations and the warm tête-à-têtes of inter-subjectivity, something like a pragmatics of thought over the long historical haul of societies. People are not influenced by words alone. Messages transmit themselves as well by gestures, by figures and pictures, the whole panoply of the sign's 'archives.'"

"To speak clearly, all in all you're connected with the history of ideas, a proven discipline you would like to apparel after the present day's tastes, after the fashion for 'communication'. . . ."

"No, not really. The theme of communication is, strictly, for-eign to my concerns. I am deliberately ignorant of what an 'idea' may be, and have taken to task the ineptitude of the very word ideology. It is only the material traces of meaning that have aggravated my attention. Something which turns the history of ideas topsy-turvy." Worsening its case, these denials would increase the intruder's chances of being promptly escorted to the borders, outside the university.

It is always a thankless and awkward task to introduce ideas using notions from which one intends to be set free. Such are the reference points acknowledged by everybody, and one surely needs after all to make oneself understood. These preliminaries, inevitably negative, oblige one to draw punctilious lines and make fastidious distinctions where until now there prevailed soothing surface continuities. An irritating business for all con-cerned parties. The study of the *ways and means of symbolic efficacy*, since such is our object, skirts either by chance or force some imposing disciplines which nourish it from many direc-tions with information and suggestions. To deal for example with the functions of visual representations and artifacts [*l'image*], art history and the history of technology have been indispensable—but insufficient. Similarly, regarding the efficacy of social ideas, we have constantly found ourselves adjoining of course *sociology*, from Weber to Bourdieu; but also the *history of mentalities*, of Georges Duby and Jacques Le Goff; or *historical psychology*, illustrated for Greek man by Jean-Pierre Vernant; or the *history of symbolism* of a Pierre Nora, centering on the col-lective effects of memory; or, besides those, the *cultural history* that Roger Chartier, Jean-Claude Schmitt, Paul Zumthor and so many others are in the process of renewing. I cite here the his-torical arsenals from where I have borrowed arms and projectiles: in order, however, if I may be so bold, to deploy them in a different research strategy. Well, in any case a subver-sive strategy, in relation to the former history of ideas, because it has to do with reversing its habitual course by substituting con-cern for its mouth or delta for concern over the *sources* of the flow. Not "what is this thought the product *of*" but "what has it effectively produced?" Not "where does this information come from and what does it mean?" but "what has this new information transformed in the mental space of this collective and its devices of authority?" Describing the development of a philosophy into a non-philosophy, of a moral science into a non-moral science, of a discourse into a non-discourse, leads to a coming to terms not with messages themselves in their literalness, not with the underlying *epistemè* of such and such a domain of utterances, but with the more obscure and trivial phenomena of processes of advance, diffusion, propagation. It is from this moment that the genesis, workmanship and content of "discourses" is effaced before their effects "below street level." Because it no longer then is a matter of deciphering the world of signs but of understanding the "world-becoming" of signs, the Churchification of a prophet's word, the scholarization of a series of seminars, the formation of a Party from a Manifesto, or Reformation from a printed poster in a public place, the "becoming-Revolution" of enlightened ideas, the "becoming-national" panic of a radio broadcast of Orson Welles in the U.S.A., or the "becoming-delivered" rice sack of a humanitarian broadcast on French television. Let us say: the "becoming-material" forces of symbolic forms.

This is not to make a religion out of the classic opposition between the *certum* and the *verum*, certitudes (commonly known) and (uncommon) truths. But my incompetencies, as much as my life's trajectory, have personally confined me to the study of the first intellectual district: that of the myths, beliefs and doctrines swallowed up for a century by the so fallacious term "ideology." It is the universe of *-isms*, or of collective affiliations founded on a proper noun (Platonism, Christianity, Marxism, Lacanism, etc.), a universe in which the potency of symbols must pass through the specific forms of power, does not get developed in the same space-time, answers not to the same exigencies of validation as the universe of *-ics* (mathematics, physics, etc.). The technologies of belief and of social being clear a field that is wider but less readily controllable than the "technologies of intelligence" Pierre Lévy has scrutinized, or "the science in action" so deftly deconstructed by Bruno Latour and the researchers of sociology of innovation from the Ecole des mines, who bring to light the unwieldy mediations—political, rhetorical, industrial—of what people take to be true. As rigorous in its effects as it is evanescent in its causalities, belief is perhaps all the more imperceptible the more easy it is to access, veiled by its familiarity and the false transparency of the train of its ideas. This is doubtlessly behind the belatedness of our knowledge of the mechanisms governing influence and the ascendancy over knowledge of the production of experimental or falsifiable truths. Compared with an epistemology already well-assured of its object and methods, a "doxology" or learnedness about non-knowledge stutters. There is no Great Wall between the two realms of observation and adhesion, between the constructed and the spontaneous, but we are more familiar with the gears and networks of science than with those of the collective imaginary. As if, in spite or because of their airiness, convictions were to us more impenetrable than the tangible results of the work of proof. As if the closed doors of laboratories offered less resistance than the banging doors of painters' studios, printshops or electronic imaging. Political hallucination remains a mystery; the physiology of vision is one no longer. We know better what we measure, and what measurement means, when we calculate the dynamic mass of a galaxy than when we quantify by polling a state of opinion. Likewise do we have more familiarity with the uses and effects of the computer, the standard tool of men and women of science today, than with those of television, daily tool and concern of today's politicos. And there are only the rarest dialogues between these two categories of objects and subjects.

It is hardly necessary to recall how the human sciences have already so amply treated the thousand circumstantial levels of signs' efficacy, affecting that symbolic mammal *homo sapiens* and *loquens*. Anthropology has shown us, exemplified by the shaman's recitations before the tribal woman in labor, how "the passage to verbal expression releases the physiological process" (Lévi-Strauss). The psychoanalyst confirms through his/her clients the virtues of the talking-cure (Freud); the sociologist of culture submits as evidence the symbolic violence practiced by the higher-ups simply through ways of saying, doing, classifying, behaving, perceiving, eating—and whose arbitrariness the lower-downs assimilate as natural (Bourdieu); the sociologist of politics knows from experience that giving the orders means transmitting and subjecting, inculcating, since domination ordinarily has no recourse to physical violence (Weber). The poets who, for their part, treated the question at the same time as the princes and well before the human sciences, on numerous occasions have exalted "the word, that force that goes" (Hugo), or further the "powers of speech" (Edgar Allan Poe). But before they came along, some nomads of the Near East had invented God in their image, lending him right from the start—Act I, Scene I—that mysterious and thus divine aptitude for transmuting an act of saying into doing: *fiat lux*, "and there was light." Enunciation = Creation. We have perhaps forgotten Genesis, but the *sensus communis* at bottom is always taken for Yahve every time it evokes not the trumpets felling the walls of Jericho but books "which break with tradition," "spoken words that caused a shock wave," "ideas that alter the face of things," etc. These colorless metaphors conceal the performative mystery by banalizing it, but one has to consciously resolve not to consider as self-evident that the spoken word of Jesus of Nazareth was able at a certain point in its course to transform the Roman Empire and give birth to Christianity; or that Urban II's preaching at Clermont, putting bands of pilgrims and entire armies into motion, brought forth the first Crusade; that the posting at Wittenberg, by a former Augustinian monk, of 95 theses in Latin could have given rise to the Reformation; that the *Communist Manifesto* originated a "Communist system." In short, the fact that a representation of the world shall have modified the state of the world, and not just its perception (a fact we hold to be something natural), is worth taking the trouble reconfiguring into a real enigma. They say philosophy is the daughter of astonishment. It is not enough just to be dumbfounded to become a philosopher, but my different works all arise out of intellectual wonder at the cliches that naturalize an even more mysterious operation than signification, namely the transition of the sign to the act. At the entry to the "black box" there are sonorities, letters, faint traces; at the exit: new legislations, institutions, police forces. To dismantle this "box" is to analyze what we shall call *a fact or deed of transmission*, or to produce the rules of transformation from one state into another (not the gaseous into the liquid, but the chain that would follow sermonizing into an army or magic book, and from that into a Party or State; or "logic into epilepsy"). The structural stability of languages and codes is one thing, the quaking of a stable structure by an event of speech or word, or any other symbolic irruption, is another.

3. Primary Definitions

Your criticism of my propositions will perhaps be facilitated by a few prefatory and summary definitions. I call therefore "mediology" the discipline that treats of the higher social functions in their relations with the technical structures of transmission. I call "mediological method" the case-by-case determination of correlations, verifiable if possible, between the symbolic activities of a human group (religion, ideology, literature, art, etc.), its forms of organization, and its mode of grasping and archiving traces and putting them into circulation. I take for a working hypothesis that this last level exerts a decisive influence on the first two. The symbolic productions of a society at a given instant *t* cannot be explained independently of the technologies of memory in use at the same instant. This is to say that a dynamics of thought is not separable from a physics of traces.

The means of routing a message, the point of passage to which it is bound, furnishes for analysis a major but limited element. The medium in the McLuhanite sense of the word is but the ground floor. One cannot thus rest there.

Objects and works count less, of course, than operations. Let us guard against the substantialist trap by integrating the *medium* as a device or system of representation [*dispositif*] into *mediation* as the actual use or disposal of resources [*disposition*]. Or, further, by integrating such and such cultural substantives—books, images—into the corresponding infinitive—*to read, to look at*—and above all into the variations of that act (the *ways* of reading and looking, their social frameworks and styles). Herein lies the inversion of hierarchies: the text as an ideal unity is less pertinent than the book as object, and the object in its turn less so than its metamorphoses. Our province is the intermediate or intercalative,* because we are much given to the intervals, intercessors and interfaces of transmission. But with the prefix *inter-* designating as it does an order of realities invariably secondary in relation to the terms it fits together, we have preferred instead the Latin suffix *-ion, -io* betokening action or process, here of technology-culture *interactions*. It is in reality the intermediate spaces and time, the betweenness of two things or periods, the trough of the wave [*les entre-deux*], that are decisive; but our language works the opposite way: it spontaneously subordinates the signs of relation to those of being, and doing to being.

The mediologist busies himself with the forms of media like Marcel Proust with his *petites madeleines*, or Sigmund Freud with his slips. No less but no more. Let us even say, relatively rarely. The word *media*, that false friend of the mediologist, denotes "any means of technical support making possible the massive diffusion of information (press, radio, television, cinema, advertising, etc.)" (*Petit Robert*). "The media" does not name in our view an autonomous, coherent field liable to be constituted into its own specific discipline. This is not only because they are overdetermined, spanning a multiplicity of determinants at once economic, technical, political, cultural, ideological, etc.—as is the case with any process of transmission—but because they are but a more particular variant, inflated yet derived from a permanent question of global principle. What was offered by Aristotle's reflections on rhetoric, or Plato's on writing and the sophist, and, quite as much as those, by the case of that original Marathon runner, seen as author and victim of the West's first "scoop"—all these matters relate not to presently fashionable mass-mediology but do come directly under the headings of our field. Contemporary media are only decrypted over the long term, in temporal depth. To begin to approach television as a mediologist and not a sociologist of communication, one needs to take up an ancestral soul and observe it in perspective, against the light surrounding the Byzantine icon,

---

*In the sense of that which is introduced to a series of already existing elements, as in the cases of the additional day of February to bring the calendar in line with the natural solar year, or a newly acknowledged geological bed (for example, associated with a period of subsidence) between two other strata, or the modifying elements tacked on to words in the development of a language to make compound words (agglutination). [Trs.]

the traditional form of painting, photography, and cinema. The moment is understood through process, as is the past through the whole.

Shall we then take as our object the *medium* in the singular? Not *that* either, except that insofar as the interposing environments of transmitting symbols are structured by a dominant medium one cannot not envisage a role for this muddled term, on condition of granting its complexity (so much does its ordinary use often prove mystifying and simplistic). In the transmitting of a message, *medium* can be understood in four non-contradictory but exclusive senses. 1. As a *general procedure* of symbolizing (the word, writing, the analogical image, digital calculation). 2. As a social *code* of communication (the natural language in which a verbal message is pronounced—say, Latin, English, or Czech). 3. As a supporting material system or surface for receiving an inscription or archiving (clay, papyrus, parchment, paper, magnetic tape, screen). 4. As a *recording device* paired with a certain distribution network (via the manual labor of scribes, print workshop, photograph, television, information systems). Let us agree on the propriety of calling "medium" in the strong sense the system of *apparatus-support-procedure*, that which a mediological revolution would unsettle and disturb organically. The general technical method of "writing," bereft of any indication of the support system enabling and conserving its markings, or of the network through which they circulate, fails to specify concretely the nature of a medium. The "writing" sign displayed on the computer screen is to our eye another medium from the same sign on the paper's surface: it has passed from the graphosphere to the videosphere. Whence notably the inadequacy of the hasty antitheses written/oral—differences in the recording surfaces and networks of distribution having been abstracted.

A mediological revolution does not fundamentally affect the extant linguistic codes (printing with presses did not change the syntax or vocabulary of French), no more than it abolishes the other modes of transmission (they continued in the sixteenth century to produce sermons and manuscripts). The invention of printing did not all by itself manufacture a new material basis for receiving graphic imprints: rag paper already existed. Nor did it create an original formal structure for binding the reading surface: the "codex" book was several centuries old at the time, and the forms of books remained for nearly a century after Gutenberg those of the manuscript, as Roger Chartier has reminded us. Nonetheless, beyond the inertia of status quo communicative activities and taking account of the periods of latency, Gutenberg's technology would prove effective in profoundly overturning, if not the modalities of reading, at least the symbolic status and social reach of the written word through mass literacy. Moveable lead type required paper, but the latter would have vegetated, so to speak, without the former. The dynamic was that of the pair lead-paper, but the true operative agency—quantitative and qualitative—of a convulsive upheaval in the sign's medieval ecology was, in the final instance, the invention of the letter-press: the motorized and matricial machine of a new anthropological structure characterized as "modernity."

Every revolution of this genre is multifactored. And it would be reductionist, obviously, to promote the medium into a unique causal agent when it remains the necessary but not sufficient condition of a mediological revolution. The machinery, in Daniel Bougnoux's words, holds in its control only half of the program; the other half is made by the milieu, and causality follows a circle. A medium is nurtured and grows through the environment, which may or may not make demands of it. And doubtless one could apply to the first hand-press and print impression the same type of assessment David Landes applies to the mechanical clock: "It is not the clock that provoked an interest for measuring time; it is the interest that led to the clock's invention."[1] Epidemiology and microbiology have illuminating ways of approaching environmental causality in this regard. Just as the variability of the virus is a function of the site into which it is introduced (the same virus that causes AIDS in humans is harmless in chimpanzees), the variability of a mediological effect is explained by the degree of resistance of the cultural and social milieu (each one having an immunological defense system *sui generis*). The same complex of

---

[1] David S. Landes, *Revolution in Time: Clocks and the Making of the Modern World* (Cambridge: Belknap Press of Harvard University Press, 1983). The need had been recognized in the monastic setting, after the Benedictine and Cistercian reforms, for a punctual daily celebration of the canonical offices.

machines can be revealed epidemic in one place and indifferent in another. The site of eleventh century China was unable to foster and fully adapt on a large scale founts of moveable characters, which knew a resurgence and growth in the fifteenth century, at the other end of the world, in passing from wood (block) to lead (type).* Chinese xylography met a modest demand for printed texts, required no heavy investment, and maintained more easily a close tie with the calligrapher's style. The Mycenaean milieu of the twelfth century B.C. had not allowed the linear phonetic notation of thought to "mature." It confined the invention to the royal precinct, in the hands of a caste of scribes, for purposes of bureaucratic regulation. The Athenian habitat reaped its benefits, a few centuries later, and transformed the procedure of keeping secret records within the palace walls into a means of publicizing laws and civic equality in the agora.

Thus the causal tie between a technology and a culture is neither automatic nor unilateral. One cannot be sure about the types of behavior that linear writing is going to develop in a given setting. Still, one can be sure that a culture unaware of this particular procedure of memorization will *not* have such and such a behavioral pattern: it will have no cognizance of how to class things, list events, place items in columnar format, etc. (And thus will have no cognizance of the logic of non-contradiction, linear history, cumulative memory, etc.). But has not the science of ecology for a long time traded in the more straightforward mechanistic causalities for "systematic" models? It is well known that it does not rain in the Sahara because there is no vegetation, and no vegetation because it does not rain. Christianity helps along the victory of the *codex* (our own form of book) over the *volumen* (or scroll), unfit for liturgical reading because so little able to be easily handled, and the victory of the *codex* helps along that of Christianity over pagan practices. Both phenomena co-produce one another.

To the "small" system of the material base, or surface of inscription along with its apparatus for making and preserving

---

*On the history of printing generally, and the Chinese precedent, see Lucien Febvre and Henri-Jean Martin, *The Coming of the Book: The Impact of Printing, 1450–1800* (London: Verso, 1976), esp. pp. 71–5. [Trs.]

signs, responds the "large" medium-milieu, a socio-technological complex that is mediology's historical object proper. "Milieu" is more than scenery or stage-effects, or than an exterior space of circulation: it conditions the semantics of traces slanted by a social organization. It sets the horizon of meaning of messages received across "the logic of custom or use" (Jacques Perriault) of which it is the porter (arranging for welcoming, withdrawing, hostility, standing-by, etc.). This "logic" is not some user code simply "in the air," an autonomous mode of implementation spread equally among a population of virtual users. Its coordinates line up with a political map of recognized competencies—in solidarity as they are with a hierarchized distribution of positions and expertises, of an organized regulation of accesses to different communicative bases and systems. A historical milieu of transmission crystallizes concretely in, and through, the socialized operators of transmission. It is a space constructed by, and upon, networks of appropriators, official guarantors of reputations, regulators, go-betweens or middle-men, etc. This holds for printing, for example, with its editor-booksellers, retailers, educators, librarians, organizers of reading rooms, administrators of provincial academies, etc. "They select, make available and control the dynamos of information; they render it desirable and assimilable, they are the active agents of its appropriation and transformation."[2] But each novel medium modifies the operative capacity and thus political importance of each of the networks already functioning. In general the new demotes the old. Each mediological revolution gives rise to its own producers of friction, its own "switch points" along the tracks of its development, and the history of a cultural milieu can be read (and written) as that of the short-circuits and competitions between juxtaposed, or rather, superposed, devices of transmission (thus with today's school networks, bookstores, presses, radio, television).

The error of futurologists and disappointment of futurists commonly arise from overestimating the *medium*'s effect by underestimating the *milieu*'s weighty plots. As a general rule, usage is more archaic than the tool. The explanation is self-evident: if the

---

[2] Michel de Certeau, Luce Giard, *L'Ordinaire de la communication* (Paris: Dalloz, 1983), p. 8.

medium is "new," the milieu is "old," by definition. It is a strati-
fication of memories and narrative associations, a palimpsest of
gestures and legends continuously prone to reactivation, the repertory we rapidly leaf through of representational structures and
symbols from all preceding ages. I am papyrus, parchment, paper,
computer screen. I am the Decalogue, François Villon, Lenin and
Macintosh. I am pictogram and alphabet, text and hypertext,
manuscript, printed page and radiating screen. It is the same with
individuals as with mediaspheres. Each mediasphere concretely
supposes heterogeneous *mediospaces*. France in the videosphere is
"a hexagon any of whose sides are only an hour and a half away,"
and whose images have the speed of light. But having Airbus and
live TV coverage has not done away with the country's depart-
mental jurisdictions originally measured as portions of space that
one can cross by horse in one day. The most recent layer of signs
reaches us through the older ones, in a perpetual re-inscribing of
the archives, such that the new takes effect in, by, and on the old.
Hence the eternal lateness of effective customary use above and
beyond the tool's potentialities, of event overtaking expectations.
Hence the tenacious viscosity of quotidian practices, the hijacking
or misappropriation and longer by-passing of the available apparatuses, and at times the felicitous surprises issuing from the
chronological *bricolage* to which any culture and individual is
constrained vis-à-vis its/his material bases of representation.

Let us sum up. In the word "*mediology*," "*medio*" says not
media nor medium but *mediations*, namely the dynamic combination of intermediary procedures and bodies that interpose
themselves between a producing of signs and a producing of
events. These intermediates are allied with "hybrids" (Bruno
Latour's term), mediations at once technological, cultural and
social. We are quite ill-prepared to deal with crossings and com-
posites. The edifice of signs divides into the three levels of the
physical (or technological), semantic, and political. But its study
has been up to the present day partitioned into air-tight disciplines: the first level attributed to "the history of sciences and
technologies"; the second, to the "sciences of culture"; the third,
to the "sciences of society." The same segmentation has applied in
professionalized practices: to the technocrats and engineers belong
cable and "cultural equipment," that is the care of the conduits; to

intellectuals and artists go the messages and significations, i.e. the care of contents; to the princes and decision-makers, at last, the monitoring of customs and the control of profits, i.e. care of the trade-offs and fall-out effects. Yet "the transition from the pure to the married state" that constitutes a symbolic utterance's entry into action does not respect those borders. Neither does mediology: it aspires to be trans-bordered, athwart establishments and nomenclatures. In order to think through what is otherwise inconceivable to it, has not each age of human reason had to confront incommensurables, find connections between whole continents? Everything takes place as if one had always unconsciously dissociated 1)the technological question—which machine is at work here? 2)the semantic question—which discourse are we given to understand? and 3)the political question—which power is exerted, how and on whom? Looking not for *that which is* behind, but for *what takes place between*, the mediologist beholds himself constrained to set up his footstool before three more dignified arm-chairs: those of the historian of technology, the semiologist and the sociologist. An uncomfortable position but inevitable. Philosophy, apart from a few exceptions, turns its back on technological modalities, and to history's variations; history turns its on the anthropological invariants, and the concepts that describe them. Sociologists turn theirs on the world of objects and technical systems; students of technology, on subjects and mentalities; and semiologists, on both of these. This is why, and for lack of any alternative, crossing fields legitimized to our way of thinking a "staggered" approach, to attempt connecting the universe of subjects with systems of objects.

The neurosciences endeavor to surmount the brain/mind breach. The study of societies until just yesterday continued to separate the machine or the tool and, on the other side, spirituality or culture; *here*, the history of technologies and *there* the "moral sciences." And rags do not mix well with napkins, under penalty of unleashing immediately the defensive attack: vulgar materialism, naive reductionism, obsolete determinism. The mixing of rubrics appears, however, indispensable for grasping the organizational logic of a political and intellectual history, but also the collective attitude of a given period, which was stigmatized in its time as "dominant ideology" where one would rather see today the "conjunctive tissue of the mind of societies" (Le Goff). The mediological manner or cast of mind consists in putting one's finger on the *intersections* between intellectual, material and social life, and in making these too silent hinges grate audibly. That is, in looking for the mainspring, the excluded third term of our grand narratives, the one that *bridges without pontificating* by connecting software and hardware. For example, an analysis of the movement of ideas in France in the eighteenth century, of interest to mediology, will favor those informal intermediate spaces, those key sites, poles of social attraction and centers of intellectual elaboration that were clubs, salons, *cénacles*, theater boxes, reading rooms, literary societies, circles, not to speak of more regular academies and institutions. The bookseller will seem more worthy of attention than literature, meeting places than commonplaces, and journalistic or café culture than the culture of literary wits. Or sellers who spread news and make reputations than the authors. The Enlightenment seen from this angle is not a corpus of doctrines, a totality of discourses or principles that a textual analysis could comprehend and restore; it is a change in the system of manufacture/circulation/storage of signs. That is, in the first appearance of nodes and networks of sociability, interfaces bearing new rituals and exercises, proving worthy as means of producing opinion. These are, in sum, through their displacement of intermediary bodies, a reorganization of the structural articulations of public spirit. It is not the ideas or the thematics of Enlightenment that determined the French Revolution, but rather that set of logistics (without which these ideas would never have take on corporeal forms).

Here is something that will sound to historians like a return to sender. What after all does the history of mentalities do, if not practice concretely, from live models, this type of approach? Was it not that which taught us to allow the interstices and residues of the events of history to begin to yield their fruits? To prefer the everyday, the automatic and the collective to the eponymous heroes and summits of social visibility? Jacques Le Goff, apropos the medieval sermon and painted or sculpted image: "Mass media are the privileged vehicles and matrices of mentalities." Roger Chartier apropos the spread of the Enlightenment: "Receptions are always appropriations that transform, reformulate, exceed what they receive." Observing this to be the case, the apprentice mediologist, who could have given himself the flashier part to play facing the history of a century ago, just as the neurochemist today opposes the old psychology of faculties, convinces himself that he has still less to bring to the historian of mentalities than the sociologist to social history. Reconstructing theoretically the empirical cases elaborated by the workings of the new history, the mediologist can at the most propose macroscopic models of conceptualization, if not explanation. The mental (which comes from *mens*, mind) tends upward; the materialities of culture downward. By ascribing the equipment of societies' *mentalités* to their technologies for domesticating space and time, we shall be able to join modestly with other "guilds" of social and human science to purposely lower the debate. This we can further do by extending to the mediological supports of those *mentalités* the allegedly reductive role imputed elsewhere to the biological bases of the psyche; as we can also do by translating "revision of values" by "displacement of vectors." A socio-analysis of the *homo academicus* cannot help not readily imputing, therefore, an alleged "aristocratism" to those contemporary philosophies that would resort to the specialists' "*-logy* effect" (grammatology, marxology, archeology, semiology, etc.) "in order to borrow the methods and appearances of the scientificity of the social sciences without giving up the privileged statute of the philosopher."[3] Far from locking ourselves into a self-sufficient and self-referential notion about universals, we prefer nothing more than immersion in the contingency of historical accidents and things, while at the same time mindful to posit or set off from the magma of events some structures of necessity of a more general character. For, instead of making note of the documentable, like the historian, the mediologist dreams of conveying reasons for things, by showing the skeletal structure beneath the flesh, what one could call "the hard of the soft." Truly, more than removing the partition between vectors and values, we would have needed to talk about strengthening crisscrossed lacings: an intertwined kind of understanding that would de-ideologize "ideologies," desanctify sanctities, but also mentalize the material bases of systems of inscription, and

[3] Pierre Bourdieu, *Réponses* (Paris: Le Seuil, 1992), p. 131.

psychoanalyze not souls but tools. That is, in one and the same gesture, make our mnemo-technic equipment intelligible as mentality and our mental equipment intelligible as technology.

4. By Invariants and Variations

Writing about the power of intellectuals, the Scribe, the Word, the history of Looking, the State—should I dare say that as a philosopher I have never produced books of anything other than history, however heavily conceptualizing they may also be. The just estimation of meaning can be treated as synchrony, after the stable ground rules of a code; but not the just estimation of effective power, which supposes a diachrony (if only in the "horse-steam engine" sense of the term: a unit of work per unit of time). It had to do in each instance, indeed, with "substituting for the autarchical analysis of structures the transversal study of a logic" (Sylvie Merzeau). How? By making a column of invariant traits, on the left, correspond to a series of pertinent variations, on the right; whence those synoptic tables for a holistic view of such and such a trajectory (see appendices). The functions in a given framework of civilization are invariant: there is a relational function of the servants of the absolute, like scribes or intellectuals; a reconstitutive function of visual images, whether one refers to it after the fashion of "scopic impulsion" or of Pascal's "image-producing faculty" (the one that "dispenses reputations and gives respect to persons"); or, the propaganda function of State power. What is variable are the regimes of the functioning. And it is the order of these fluctuations that this double-entry grid or template would want to produce.

We were not in pursuit of identities but passages and emergences (thus arose our interest in those watersheds, the sixteenth and twentieth centuries). Comparatism (not between cultures here, but phases) worked loose and brought to light the significant differences. This does not throw into relief a general anthropology, since the exercises of power and practice have priority over structures and the cross-sectioned trajectory. Nor does it clear the way to a positive (or positivist) history, because the pertinent variations are related back to invariants and we seek not only to establish but to order them. The ideal project would have been to assay a techno-history of culture, to be brought one day under a historical anthropology here and there presently taking shape.

The "techno-" is upstream from or at the heart of the "socio-." This is what immediately set off the approach taken here in relation to the sociologist. One encounters it clearly in the example of how a culture looks at art and symbols, and in the history of that looking. In "A Median Art, Essay on the Social Uses of Photography," the sociological interest focuses on the behavioral codes and modes of appropriation of the medium. The sociologist demonstrates extremely well how the characteristics of the photograph as an objective imprint of things fulfill the expectations of popular naturalism. This innovative work that consists of "regaining an objectified sense produced from the objectification of subjectivity" takes for granted, however, what is singular to the *recorded* image which distinguishes it radically from the "icon" and "symbol" form. It subjects to no examination the invention's disruptive effects on the previous or bordering practices of representation: print engraving and painting. And thereby leaves intact the whole genealogy of representative technologies in which one would observe the medium-photograph overthrowing by degrees the economy of visual messages. It goes without saying that no single angle of view on photography disqualifies another, the counter-field of mediology coming eventually to complete the sociological field, without claiming for itself, latecomer that it is, the same norms of knowledge.

More vulnerable to the unexpected than his distinguished neighbors, the mediologist continues on his way from one surprise to the next in the adventurous history of inventions.[4] The technological object puts him out of countenance; each innovation would nearly force him to change theories. The sociologist, the semiotician or the psychoanalyst tend to great technological emergences indiscriminately, as these theoreticians are in the bosom of an already constructed system of a prioris. They hasten

[4] The last sentence uttered by d'Arago when presenting the daguerreotype at the Academy of Sciences, in 1839: "In this genre, it's on the unexpected that one must particularly rely."

to show that, be their object animal, mineral or vegetable, it confirms their set of preexistent rules—the war between the classes, the system of the code, or the topic of psychological instances. Have not these disciplines become much too sure of themselves to recall Apollinaire's advice to the poet: "Mind a train does not come along and no longer surprise you"? They most often reduce the new artifact to the state of a metaphor of themselves. Far from exclaiming something to the effect of "that's it exactly, see for yourself," the mediologist of how artifacts have been looked at, when faced with an African idol, a museum painting, a photograph, the cinema, television, begins with a "that's not 'it' at all, I no longer recognize myself in it." "But it's very simple!" says the already constituted systematic branch of knowledge to itself, knowing all in advance. "That gets more and more complicated," muses the other.

To learn meant, in an earlier time, to simplify, by finding the simple intelligible invariant of complicated empirical variations. Peirce established in this way that the semiotic world, or "semiosphere," is distinguished from the organic, or biosphere, by the mediation of an "interpretant." It is this third term between the sign and the object which does not exist in the reflexive sequence of stimulus-response. Here is a tertiariness that betokens human freedom: let us see in it an anthropological invariant. I cannot make it such that my lower leg does not kick if one gives it a light tap above the knee, but I can run a red light, smile at someone who gives me a chilly welcome, or decline a gesture of friendship addressed to me. A "semiotic situation" leaves me free as to my responses, including not responding. But this space of freedom is not a space of indifference, a subjective indetermination independent of the nature of the "semaphores" at our disposal. One cannot, for example, fit modern "mass communications" into an ahistorical conceptual framework, a sort of state of nature of culture, and call the latter *the* prevailing situation of semiosis" or semiosphere. It is one thing to understand our "mass culture" actuality in accordance with a model of intelligibility, as the token is to the type or the phenomenon to the structure. It is another to dissolve the one in the other. A simplification that no longer allows one to identify the historical differences—for example, between the "semiosic situations" of the archaic Greek world, the Christian Middle Ages, or of our twenty-first century—ceases to be operative in order to become comfortable. Hence the necessity of a second level of time for the act of knowing: to introduce some discontinuousness within a continuity. To concretize the abstract universality "the semiotic situation" constitutes is to state it more specifically as a *mediasphere*, a concrete variation of the atemporal invariant *semiosphere*. Here the principle of intelligibility of the empire of signs is but the same thing as its periodization. Time is needed in order to understand, and above all to understand *what one says*, as I remember Althusser reminding us one day. There is neither a synoptic table nor a distinction made among mediaspheres in my *The Scribe* and *Teachers, Writers, Celebrities*; but it is indeed the difference in the shift from the French scholar-intellectual [*clerc*] to the monk that personally set me on the "mediological" path, by hindering me from choosing—in defining the "intellectual," (a task become our national *pons asinorum*)—between the historical and structural approaches. Certainly in the France of today, what presents itself to view is but a milieu of sociability structured by three poles: university, publishing-editing, medias. And certainly these poles *co-exist* in any given one of them and at present, with all sorts of well-known connecting bridges between them. But each predominant, successively central space of attraction can be historically dated. 1880 to 1930 concentrated the university cycle; 1930 to 1968, the editorial cycle; 1968 to who knows when, the mediatic cycle. Three cycles that also are good for "recyclings," whereby what is recycled is a "clerical-intellectual" function that preceded the birth of the very word and of the secular intelligentsia (see Le Goff: *Les Intellectuels au Moyen Age*), and will outlive it should need for that prove to be the case. Here, the invariant function appears as soon as one passes from substantive definition of "the intellectual" as "the man of ideas and values" to his operative definition as "the man of the transmitting" (of ideas and values). It is the function that determines the status and not the reverse. To aim at the exact nature of functions practiced in reality, rather than at the official untitledness of print organs and so on, makes apparent a logic of the places occupied by these functions which does not correspond to the logic of signs and insignia. It involves a change of the angle

of vision producing this slightly preposterous idea that the journalistic institution fulfills a social function not all that different
from the secular clergy long ago: the mediative as the functional
"ecclesiastical" of the moment. It is no longer the homily from
the pulpit but the narration of the news on screen and paper that
presently provides for the translation of event into symbol and of
peripeteia or mere incident into dramatic art. Each "menu," each
page layout, is a lay sermon (or moral instruction), with its hierarchy of titles, and thus of events and persons, with its
providential logic of meaningful sequences or imputed chains of
cause and effect, its allegorical use of photographs, etc. (The
basic journalist, to continue the homiletic metaphor, is the parish
priest of old; the editorial director, an archbishop; the news-
reader or anchorperson, with all of France's hexagon as
jurisdiction, a primate of the Gallican church. Hence that moot
question of mediology, let it be noted in passing: the debate over
ordaining women in the catholic world, a debate already settled
technologically while the Vatican's back was turned.)

The question "why convey, why transmit meanings" [*pourquoi
transmettre*] comes under the heading of an anthropology; the
question of "what there is *to* transmit," under that of an ethics;
the question of "how does one transmit" under that of a historical mediology. At least let us say that while the function of
symbolic mediation *is* orderable into categories, *is* transhistorical,
anchored in the theorem of incompleteness as the transcendental
condition of collective organization, the institutional organs of
this function are precarious, singular, ever-changing. One must
take them on as a historian and no longer as a philosopher. But
this is only the initial exodus. To understand the structuring of
the historical succession of institutional organs by the technological evolution of the material bases of representations and
systems of inscription [*supports*], conventional historical
accounts do not suffice. There is a need to make oneself a technologist—or put clearly, given the nature of the means in
question, a mediologist. A second exodus, or the further exile
within exile already from the concept. For a metaphysician there
is little brilliance in what the historian does. And just as little, for

a simple historian, in what the historian of technology does, despite the exhortations of Lucien Febvre and Marc Bloch. This drop by two degrees in rank—if we hold to the venerable hierarchies knowing full well how outmoded they are—was included in the logic that reasoned: first, to understand the *opus*, look toward its *operation*; second, to understand the operation, look toward the *equipment* or *apparatus*; third, to understand these things, look toward the *series* in which they take their place. And this is how a study like my *Teachers, Writers, Celebrities* or even more *A History of the Western Eye* is sure to seem too anecdotal in the philosopher's view, and too systematic in the historian's. The latter distrusts totalizing concepts, experienced as he is in the complexities of practices. The former spurns the singularities of empirical history because to describe variations without giving their reason seems to him uninteresting. Sensitive to where these two oppositely posed objections have validity, the mediologist (and this is to be feared) will escape neither.

5. What is a Mediasphere?

In these small critical histories (that historians will doubtlessly determine to be "philosophical"), the chronological unifier can be called the *mediasphere, or middle ground, setting or environment* [milieu] *of the transmission and carrying* [transport] *of messages and people*. This *milieu*, structured by its foremost technique and practice of memory-formatting, structures in its turn a type of accrediting of the discourses in currency, a dominant temporality, and a mode of grouping together that are the three faces of a trihedron forming (what one could sum up as) the collective personality or psychological profile proper to a mediological period.

Historically, every mediasphere is specific to time and place, and our tables (see appendix) distinguish between three primary types: the *logosphere*, when writing functions as the central means of diffusion under the constraints and through the channels of orality; the *graphosphere*, when printed text imposes its rationality on the whole of the symbolic milieu; the *videosphere*, with its devitalization of the book via audiovisual media. This succession does not encompass, it will be noted, periods and societies without writing systems: it is properly speaking historical (post-Neolithic). This limitation pertains only to our object of study. One of the key references we have consulted, the ethnologist Jack Goody, has thematized by working from surveys conducted in Sub-Saharan Africa the exit of cultures from what could be called the *mnemosphere*, or oral transmission founded exclusively on the arts of memory. The three main effects of the written notation of thought are known: accumulation, permanent setting down of traces [*fixation*] and their depersonalization. Writing inaugurated the transmission of the symbol *at a distance*, in space and time, and on this head can serve as our chronology's far-end buffer zone. We have confined inquiry to the passage from hand-written and oral public communication (logosphere) to the mechanical reproduction of text (graphosphere) and, following that, to the analogical—and not long thereafter, computer-graphic—recording of sonorous and visual signs (videosphere).

The combination transmission/transportation makes peri-odization a problem because to the caesura of printing's effects on memorization corresponds no equivalent caesura of effects on locomotion. The concordance of the tele-communicative and transportational, which is not only a chronological coincidence, begins with the technological and social use of electric energy (the social break coming between ten and thirty years behind the technological invention). The dates show it: to the electromagnetic telegraph corresponds the railroad, to the telephone the automobile, to radiotelephony the airplane (or to radio's years aircrafts' years), to television the intercontinental missile and space rocket launcher. But before this and for three thousand years, on the ground, the saddled horse aligned the speed of cir-culating messages with that of persons. Travel time for a long while remained stationary, if not unchanging. Simple horse-pulled wagon, passenger stagecoach, the deluxe covered carriage with suspended chassis [*carrosse*], the more elaborate public coach generally drawn by five horses [*diligence*], the sleeker hooded and windowed landau or *berline*, the barouche or calash [*calèche*] with folded black top, the lightweight one-horse, two-wheeled cabriolet or "convertible" with folding leather hood: lightening the vehicles and improving the roads shortened the delays, but without changing the unity of time (in 1650 the Paris-Toulouse route was covered in 330 hours and by 1848 in 80 hours). Even if it took but three days (and nights) for news of the Saint Bartholomew's Day massacre to reach Madrid, Julius Caesar traveled at the same pace as the prince of Condé, and Chateaubriand's Italian voyage hardly went much faster than Montaigne's. And the growing difference between transporting on the backs of men and transportation by wheel, between carrying messages or packages and changing locations, was not yet culturally significant. Putting aside the rudimentary systems of signalization by sight or sound (lighthouses and floating beacons or buoys, towers and lights, church bells and horns), the uncoupling and estrangement between the respective range of activities of the message and the messenger becomes operative only with the Industrial Revolution. It begins at the end of the eighteenth century, at the same moment as the steam engine, with the optical telegraph; and seriously, radically, in the middle of the nineteenth century, with the electromagnetic telegraph.* The instantaneity/ubiquity of messages proper to the videosphere goes back in fact to 1848.

To give back to a mentality's milieu its indissoluble configuration in space and time, it may perhaps be necessary to acknowledge the properly mediative functions of territoriality. A mediasphere is a mentality's relation to physical space as well as time. One does not communicate with God just anywhere, for example, but through the joint mediation of certain privileged sites with a certain milieu receiving travellers (shrines and places of pilgrimage). The immobilized human body does not encounter the same symbolic needs as the body of the traveller on foot or on horseback. I was able in *Cours de médiologie générale* to point out only in passing the link that existed between the appearance of monotheism and itinerancy in a desert habitat, the great period of pastoral nomadism (pp. 245–250). Relations among the Hebrews to the Invisible were mediated by a space polarized

---

*A detailed discussion of optical telegraphy or the so-called Chappe system, which operated in France continuously from 1794 to 1855 (before its supercession by electromagnetic telegraphy), can be found in Alexander J. Field's "French Optical Telegraphy, 1793–1855: Hardware, Software, Administration," *Technology and Culture*, vol. 35, no. 2 (April 1994), pp. 315–47. [Trs.]

between desert and ecumenicity [from Greek οικονμεση, Latin *oecumenè*, 'the inhabited world'], mountain and plain, as by a certain type of migration. Religious space is never isotropic: poly-theistic territoriality—of a perimetric and ponderous type closed off to wondering—is not monotheistic space, which is at once hypercentralized in representation (O Jerusalem) and delocalized (no altar).[5] Similarly the theological debate over idols, waged by iconoclasts and iconodules, cannot be detached from the debate about movable versus immovable property, portable objects ver-sus those that must remain in one place, the lightweight versus heavy or inert. Not by accident is the desert theme common to both Protestantism and Judaism, with all its practices of salva-tion—ascent, return, retreat, refuge. In the same measure that forgetting the desert and a prolonged sedentariness exposed the faithful to a relapse into idolatry, deterritorialization induced a state or rather resumption of messianic consciousness. Space, in terms of the lived relation to a geography as much physical as moral, would thus be classed among our guiding embodiments of study. And this relation indeed depends as much on the means of transportation as of transmission. Their changes of speed modify attitudes of thought as well as regimes of authority: kinetics and symbolics are in league with each other. A mediasphere's space is not objective but trajective. It would therefore be necessary to hazard the term "mediospace," the relation of a given surface area to a duration. The "ball of earth" as a mediospace of the graphosphere is not the same as that of the videosphere. The one has a circumference of three years (Magellan) and the other of twenty-four hours (Airbus).

Every subject/object dichotomy, every spirit/matter duality, would thus be fatal for a realistic perception of the mediasphere, which is as much objective as subjective. A devised system and a systemic disposition, a behavior and a representation, a mindful machinery and a mechanical mentality, properly apprehending the mediasphere activates the connecting dash within the

---

[5] I was pointing this out as a matter for conjecture, without even being cognizant of the allusions of Ernest Renan. The geographer Jean-Luc Piveteau has effectively con-solidated the hypothesis in his "La territorialité des Hébreux, l'affaire d'un peuple il y a longtemps ou un cas d'école pour le IIIe millénaire," *L'Espace géographique*, 1993, no. 1.

"techno-cultural." The calibration of social time is clearly supported here by a technological scansion, but a mediasphere is not only a technological environment. Its analysis, in the way of a psychosomatics of the social body, keeps to that borderland of collective psychologies where machines become culture and culture machinery. The proof of this is that a mediological revolution, stirring together concrete things and myths, crystallizes at the same time around an apparatus and a fetish. For the new, soon to be institutionalized, organ—promoted to its position at the center of symbolic transmissions, a sacred tool, the new mainstay of the logistics of influence, and a bearer of ambivalent affects—comes straightaway to speak in our ears an Aesopian tongue. So it was with the alphabet, the printing press, television, or the computer (soon to fuse into one single appliance). The "inert" instrument has a soul from the word go, one that confers on it the imaginary investment needed to make it a *mediabolical* organ, the ubiquitous centerpiece of our dreams of salvation and other wishes upon a star—demonic for some, for others wondrous. Each mediasphere has its frights and castles in the air. It can be as oneiric as it is mechanizing.

If technology's material base surrounds itself with a fabulous halo (which can even predate its effective public appearance, as we saw with the computer in the post-World War II U.S.), it remains no less true that the mythology fades once the material product of its performance declines in significance. The myth of the Book as the Temple of God and Emancipator of humankind failed to withstand the marginalization of the printed book by the new bases of inscription. And the old mythic investiture was carried over to the micro-computer, which is variously held to promise world salvation, promote grass-roots democracy, ensure universal "cosmopedagogy" (or the permanent education of the human species). The mythical primacy is dislodged with the practical return on investment; social status rewards the utensil-value of the tool, and not the opposite. The fact that in the mediasphere objective should not be separated from subjective cannot therefore obscure the ultimate supremacy of base over symbol. Be it the slightest letter of the alphabet, the meanest lead-typeface character, or the minutest silicon chip, the lower-case will draw in the upper-cases, sooner or later. A culture or social tradition finally earns the

fate of the devices of memory that back it up, and each new mediasphere short-circuits the class of hegemonic mediators issuing
out of its predecessor. It is hence always good mediological method
to come up with the little "whatsit" behind the lofty word that
hides it from view (translating, for instance, yesterday's "glorious
alliance of workers and intellectuals" by the hookup of the boiler
machine to the typesetter's printing case). Not only to be cured of
linguistic substantialism, in one's head, but to orient oneself correctly in life: the dynamics are on the side of the object. We have
seen that a sublime religion's birth can be apprehended as a mythic
sublimation of the setting of an original displacement. *A fortiori*,
"ideology" could be defined as the play of ideas in the silence of
technologies. Soul is the idea of the body, said Spinoza. Would not
mentality be the idea of the mediasphere?

But hardly does one utter such a formulation before having a
mind to retract it, as if the phantom of a kind of "organic totality" in the Hegelian style were paying us a visit. Let us conceive
it rather as a space of dispersion, without reduction to the homogeneous. The temptation needs resisting to draw together all the
planes of this techno-historical category around a unique center,
as happens with the "spirit of the age" or "mind of a people"—
the *Zeitgeist* and *Volksgeist* of the philosopher from Jena. Here
the unitotality would be reflected not in a spiritual principle,
but in an internal material principle. The risk would be, in sum,
substituting for the Hegelian identity of meaning and life the
identity of technology and mind as pure self-consciousness of the
technological world. Such an immanence of right into fact would
be the bearer of a *technodicy*, a profane and profanatory theod-
icy telling us that, being what everything is, technology is always
right. It would *be* Reason, with no external standpoint from
which to judge it. The history of technological development
would then become the world's tribunal. We would answer this
by noting there is no conceptual or moral dramaturgy, no majes-
tic tableau of humanity on the march to its glory, nor even any
dialectical principle busy at work in the succession of mediaspheres. It is impossible to make technological history enact the
role of philosophical history, and to presuppose that "technology
governs the world" as "Reason governs the world." For the
Hegelian Reason knows where it is going, and cannot get lost. It

leads to its realization in Absolute Spirit, disconnected from any external tie, in the autonomous plenitude of a perfectly finished freedom. Does it need recalling that scientific-technological progress is not the progressive epiphany of Liberty? It is no more the bearer of something better than of something worse: of the order of a fact, it is foreign to the order of value.

We might, it is true, have drawn other items from other tool boxes; borrowed, for example, from sociology the notion of field, because "in the field there are struggles and thus history" (Bourdieu). What can be likened to a biosphere of mind or ideality could actually mask the interplay of conflicts and competitions, shrink the margins of initiative in which those who direct symbols, as well as their personal responsibility and the political coefficient of the operations, processing, and transactions. Why not opt for the word "system," with all it implies of self-organizing and self-regulation? Or "structure," which postulates as well the immanence of a self-developing process? Instead it would seem that, contrary to all that is implicit in a structure, a mediasphere has no transhistorical essence, evolving with and as the technological sequence. Differing equally from a system, it cannot be fully isolated from its predecessors: there is no (or less and less) pure mediasphere, only one interwoven with preceding ones. And unlike the *field*, it would be sympathetic but unrealistic, so we believe, to assume that "its structure is defined by the state of the relations of force between the players" (Bourdieu). Though there be some "play" or freedom of movement across neutral space in a mediasphere too, and thus, quite fortunately, fields of opposing forces, "sphere" and "fields" are not exclusive, but rather the first englobes the second. It suggests the interdependence of elements and dependence by inclusion. On the one hand we are subjugated to a mediasphere (and not to a field) by the fact alone of being *within it*, subjugated to a system of constraints existing "independently of consciousnesses and individual wills." A sphere has a strong autonomy. On the other hand, we are bound by it to globalize our perception by reintegrating a given assemblage of tools and machinery [*appareillage*] into a cohesive "landscape." This coherence avoids the problem of having to atomize the techno-epistemic complex into loose units, by isolating them at once from their complements and their context of usage. Within the graphosphere at its zenith, the book is inseparable from public instruction, the latter from the public library, the public library from the daily press, etc.: these interdependencies speak to the new-found autonomy of the phenomenon of written materials (altogether different from isolated "graffiti" or the inscribed dedication). The "sphere" extends the visible system of the medium to the invisible macrosystem that gives it meaning. We see the microwave oven but not the immense grid of electric power it is plugged into. We see the automobile but not the highway system, gasoline storage facilities, refineries, petroleum tankers, no more than we see the factories and research installations upstream and all the maintenance and safety equipment downstream. The wide-bodied jet hides from view the planetary spider's web of the international civil aviation organization, of which it is but one strictly teleguided element. To speak of the videosphere is to be reminded that the screen of the television receiving signals is the head of a pin buried in one home out of millions, or a homing device, part of a huge organization without real organizers—of a character at once social, economic, technological, scientific, political—much more, in any event, than a network of corporate controlled production and programming of electronic images.

Just as we cannot perceive—or perceive badly—that which makes perception possible, we hardly discern spontaneously the structure of bones from which depends an era's symbolic flesh, hidden beneath the finish of its literary, aesthetic, or legal monuments.

When we read the missives of Voltaire, or of Madame de Sévigné, do we think about the services for delivering correspondence and messages they suppose? Namely: 1) a strong central power, capable of maintaining a network of roads, postal relay stations, an organization of paid permanent employees, and 2) horses to ride, thus stud farms to produce them, and thus, in the end, a military calvary. This bucolic, pacific and so widely scattered literature required armed forces and a centralized State.

When as literary critics we study the nineteenth century novel or *feuilleton*, how often do we think about the Stanhope press, the penny newspaper, the national network of schooling, and the railroads that all supported the demand for this literary form? When as historians of ideas we examine the import of socialist doctrines, how often do we think about lead typography or about the typographical milieu where these doctrines saw the light of day? Do we put socialism and Linotype printing into relation—two phenomena, after all, the duration of whose lives coincided chronologically?

The notion of a "sphere" has some serious drawbacks, but also a certain virtue of demystification. We fetishize objects isolated against their background, visible to the naked eye; networks are less easily turned into myth. Competitions and shows are held to celebrate the elegance of the automobile, but the public does not break into spontaneous rejoicing over the Highway Department. Paeans are sung over Bugattis but not tarmac. Eight-cylinder engines have been the stuff of dreams; road-menders, never.

I am acutely conscious of having exaggerated the relative autonomy of mediaspheres (and, on a smaller, more provincial scale, those of the cycles of intellectual power in France). This has been in the interest of exposition. I am not unaware that whatever clarity proffered by these dichotomies (of the written/oral type) or by these tripartitions (as in our ternary tables in the appendix) can often prove illusory. Highlighting divisions yields increased meaning or interpretive force, but to the detriment of the nuances, shadings, and finer points: it is the well-known weakness of strong oppositions. I believe, however, in the pedagogical utility of provocative schematic tabulations aiming to *visualize* a differential logic synchronically, even if it turns out that this black/white thinking leads historians (those killjoys when it comes to deep conceptualizing) to remind systematic spirits that societies prefer gray. A chart of oral and written traditions opposing feminine to masculine values, rural to urban, etc., will justly elicit reproach from the competent historian that there exists from as early as the eighteenth century a feminine literature (private, aristocratic, written and circulated by hand) and that urban "public" writing did not prevent production of the private, notarial, confiscated writing of the country provinces. These irrefutable objections do not annul, in our humble opinion, the interest of bringing to the fore the great polarities of our culture, holding true for types and archetypes; and we will simply have to learn to live with it if these diverse symmetries and classifications feed others' reservations toward mediology as a *grand délire* of synthesizing, in the scientistic mode of the nineteenth century (see appendices).

Still more grave would be the illusion fostered by the linear order of language—the illusion of a unique and linear time in which the before and the after would parade by in succession and without ever going back. This evolutionist legacy of the past century has not held up against concrete observation of societies. And the history of the sciences itself, showing signs of fluctuation and turbulence in the rivers of knowledge, confirms the idea that time flows backward as much as ever onward.[6] These recursive curlings, these spiralings in reverse, are as much marvels as sources of dismay in our cultural history. Mediaspheres have not succeeded one another as substitutions, but rather as complications in a perpetual game of mutual reactivation. Let us think "succession" more in terms of the staggered stages of the ziggurat than the linear suite of doorways or enfilade of trees. There is, to be sure, no zero sum game between written and oral, there being several sorts of writing and orality—primitive or ritualistic, individual or collective, brought about or not by a reading out loud, etc. Distinctions have been drawn between oralities that are *primal* among peoples without writing, *fundamental* in Antiquity, mixed or *secondary* in the Middle Ages (after the advent of the Holy Book), *tertiary* with radio and television. And the computer terminal, like the fax machine, renews the practices and prerogatives of the written word (even while diminishing its symbolic stature). Because we have been unconscious victims of the cruel objectivity of mechanically recorded memories (since no traces of recorded sound were ever conserved prior to the beginning of the century), as well as of the overvaluation of written text and the

---

[6] Michel Serres, preface to *Éléments d'histoire des sciences* (Paris: Bordas, 1989).

folkloric heroization of the oral (what has redundantly been called today's "verbal words"), we simply have not placed enough emphasis on the immense sub-base of the more spontaneous manifestations of living speech [*la parole vive*]. There is no meaning except by means of letters and figures. With his *La Raison des gestes dans l'Occident médiéval*, Jean-Claude Schmitt has composed a suggestive inventory of this originary dialectic between body and mind. On the ocean of signs, human beings have continued to navigate by the aural and gestural—in the margins or hollow spaces of alphabets, so to speak, or by passing over them. Yet perhaps this newly ancillary role of the written word, proper to the logosphere and which the graphosphere had virtually forgotten, will become familiar to us once again within our videosphere's formidable resurrection of gesture, voice, and teletransmitted physical presence. For we are surely rediscovering the values of the bodily that so amply feed our growing incapacity for impersonal life (and which print culture's delegation of meaning used to keep alive).

"Orality," notes Paul Zumthor in *La Lettre et la voix*, "is an abstraction; voice alone is concrete." Sign effects were first voice effects. Effects of the solar plexus, stomach, whole body, as the vocal gesture engages (more than the mouth and face) a certain poise of the upper body, stamping of the feet, movement of the arms. We should like to have evoked, along with the logosphere's historians who have done so, the primordial vibration of the stentor. And evoke too, along with the ethnologists of African cultures, that first principle of life that puts in movement all the powers contained in man, in order to dispel the bad and call forth the good. *Not* words of intimacy, the babbling near the running fountain, the murmur of hearts in unison that a Rousseauist ear would long to hear back at their origins, before the disheartening misfortunes of separation, before reparation of the first divorce by the Social Contract. *Nor* the lulling and intoxicated words of folklore, the stammered out remains "let fall from obscure catastrophes." But instead words of authority, sacral, seminal, inaugural words, malediction or benediction, bewitchment or prayer, that canopy our talk fests and our chit-chat. Or the speech of God, the verbal *primum mobile* of Genesis, of Adam in Paradise giving existence to animals and things and a person by naming them. The word of the Father inseminating the immaculate Virgin's womb without further ado or paternity suit. Sacramental, liturgical, propitiatory or comminatory words, the very breath of truth and bearers of salvation. Words by whose virtues Buddha, Pythagoras, Jesus, or Socrates (and Saussure, let us add in passing) were forever exempted from writing—and we put forever in their debt through the fading echo of their voice. Words gathered humbly, haltingly, by the ink of holy books, which are not deciphered alone but listened to in groups, in prayer, because they are believed to *carry over* the spirit or afflatus, the breath, of origins. The words of Saint Francis of Assisi and God's *jongleurs*, those with which almost all the Latin thinkers of Christianity—orators, pastors, and advocates of their order— made do; those that even today are still chanted in psalmody at night during the Byzantine holy offices of Mount Athos. Words that, somewhere between charm and charisma, rang out in the incantation of the witch doctor or exorcist spellbinding or healing their listeners; that worked in rhythm with the repetitive motions of the artisan's hands in the clay; that were pronounced by bard, *aoidos*, and *skald*, by blind itinerant Homer and a spiritualistic Hugo. Words of the master alchemists and great secrets; but also (if we go down a floor) the word of the judge who "says the law," of the magistrates who institute it, discuss it or divulge it by petition, deposition, and sentence. The vocal act of the king who ordains or promulgates the law, the herald who proclaims the edict, or Antigone who stands up and says no. Of whoever is called to hold out their hand today and swear, whoever swears by or appeals to their own private gods or their grandmother.

To these we can add the physical act of elocution that impels a taking down or taking away under its dictation and gives dictators sway over crowds subjugated by a pacing of delivery, a tone or timbre, a texture of voice. But also those words knitted into virtually the entire life of the spirit in the Middle Ages, by the university *disputatio*, by commentary and oral reading (when reading meant melodic mouthing of the words to oneself alone or in a group); as well as by those words of the liberal arts, grammar and rhetoric (with taking down notes, or *reportatio*, becoming part of the curriculum in the course of the thirteenth century, which was greeted with the strongest suspicion). Those historians who today are rehabilitating the disgraced literatures of voice (tales, romanceros, *chanson de gestes*, *fabliaux*, the songs of jongleurs, and ballads), have shown how the art and content of medieval manuscripture were deeply enmeshed in habits of orality. During more than a millennium, "to write" meant to dictate (there were no signed original manuscripts in France, it seems, before 1350). Written words held to be most valuable were *transcribed* words. Writing's sacralization may perhaps have been a kind of "backwash" of the human voice, via a borrowing and printed trace of that first proffered utterance that was at once internal to each of God's creatures and coextensive with Creation. "In the beginning was the Word" has no need of replacement by an "In the beginning was Action," for they are synonyms. A living tongue of fire, the Word is the original Energy. Concentrated in the same word are *Logos*, reason; *Pneûma*, the breath of life; and *Dynamis*, potency. The fiery pentecost was there from the Advent, just as the image was in the first graphic signs, the bull's head in the *aleph* and the house in the *beth* (making "alphabet"). In the animistic logosphere, the hieroglyph haunts the letter as the sacred the profane. And the ancient figurations of fantastic alphabets—letter-beasts, letter-flowers, letter-men—give witness to this long magic relation to writing as the deposit of divine words.

It is not, of course, to this supernatural orality that we have come back in our own latter day of the audiovisual and its leap over the cults of the written word. But our modern technological equipment of the voice once again advantages conviction more than argumentation, pragmatic relation more than logical content. The new oral culture readjusts the role of printed traces, whose efficiency and marvels seem on the wane. Much as the video-image grants a new life, in another form, to the idolatries from before the birth of art, vocal prostheses (telephone, radio, cassettes) give back to the vibrations of immediate presence a primacy that had receded. These technologies have substituted song, a warm and popular form of audio-poetry (which the primitive epic also typified), for the graphosphere's written text of poetry, which students in grade school still learn in bits but forget soon after, and which in its chilliness no longer stirs the public at large. Victor Hugo's phrase "this will do away with that" describes the effect of a mediasphere number 2 on a mediasphere number 1, but the expression reverses direction from 3 back to 1 in changing to a "this revives that" (the decay of the great monuments of writing reviving a taste for the great monumental systems of writing, within that zero-sum game Hugo suggests of equating edifice with book). So too does the philologist witness word processing on the computer stepping back over the stable identity of the text that emerged out of the modern book to rediscover the "joyous excess" of medieval copyists.[7] 3 is always closer to 1 than to 2. In urban space, at intersections or train stations, functional written text is giving way to ideograms and even pictograms of international readability. "Transalphabetical" visual forms answer with a strange echo to the pre-literate thought of Aztec or prehistoric mythograms, with their resplendent and multi-dimensional space. A reorientation along the line of the Flesh given new life by our modern illiteracy of all-image-and-sound shows a return of the "cultures of childhood" and instinctual motivating archaisms prior to the printed word. And so techno-economic globalization gives rise to the planet's politico-cultural balkanization, driving entire continents back to a pre-national, quasi-feudal fragmentation. It is as if the principle of constancy applied whereby whatever was lost from one hand was won back from the other. The fixation with the image-rich land and those centripetal values attached to it (identity- and origin-myths) come back in the fullness of the aerial and centrifugal videosphere, within and *through* it. Technological uprooting from the traditional *pagus* (*pagus* being both the page of written words and the farmer's field) has been furthered by the computer screen and the electronic stock exchange, and is offset by a religious and political reterritorialization of mentalities. Technological evolution, we have said, has nothing of the eschatological odyssey about it; but recalling that the logosphere imagined eternal beatitude as a concentration of auditory joys—angelic choirs, canticles, harps, crystalline springs and songs of birds—we can appreciate how much the graphosphere had distanced itself from paradise, and how close we are moving toward it. Was not Eden an idea brought from the Near East, the dream of a closed garden as only

[7] Bernard Cerquiglini, *Éloge de la variante: Histoire critique de la philologie* (Paris: Le Seuil, 1989).

the desert could conceive? Well beyond the conventional pictures of God's kingdom, by making out of the Word its Supreme Being, the logosphere corresponded to an "orientalization" of the Western world. And the graphosphere (which hinged archive to letter) corresponded to a counter movement of Europeanization of the non-Latin periphery, where thinking's notation by images held sway. The videosphere could see, conversely, a Far Easternization of the European, linear and alphabetical worlds. The digitization of artificial memories indeed demolished the distinction made by Peirce between icon and sign. Binary coding records ideograms as fast and as well as letters because it treats the text as an image. It brings to an end the "reproductive handicap" of East Asian figurative notations, with their thousands of ideograms so severely penalized by the requirements of printing (and by the old-style typewriter). Gutenberg had bestowed on the poor Latin alphabet, with its twenty-four signs, a serious advantage for evolving and expanding. Standardizing written form by the pixel and instant optical recognition, turning all graphic signs into equivalent visual contrasts, serves Asia more than the West. Japan, which places a premium on digitization, has as well become the best if not only producer of cameras, photocopiers, and scanners.[8] The switching places of the planet's center and peripheries, a cruel trick of the larger historical development of things, is vouched for by the humble history of reprography.

---

[8] See Michel Melot, "Photographie et intelligence artificielle," *La Recherche photographique*, numéro spécial, 1989, pp. 61–4.

II

A New Turn?

The method sketched here in broad strokes has hardly been embraced by a generous criticism, with some rare exceptions. I alone am responsible for the inadvertence, as much through my writings' intemperance—uselessly polemical or lyrical—as through the shortcomings of my knowledge. Then again, our present disciplinary segregations and the somewhat raw realism of the analysis have contributed more than a little. Add to this backdrop a certain undeserved or inappropriate notoriety associated with the author, and it is inevitable that rumor shall have oversimplified things. "Conversation," said Alain, "is always brought down to the level of the least intelligent." It has seen fit to register these labors under the social rubric "Information and Communication," when it has not lumped them under a self-confident semiology of communication at peace with its presuppositions. The only inconvenience in this is that we are at opposite ends of the earth from semiology and far removed from "Infocom."

1. Vast Misunderstanding

If one looks at them closely, not one of the problems raised in this study is conceivable within the received categories of "communication." This cancerous term, whose metastases are as precipitate as they are ungovernable, errs in our view not only by its undue *extension* to everything and anything, in its use, but also by intrinsic improprieties, in the very way it is *understood*—all of which has gradually led us to lend to the facts of material transmission an independent status.

Contemporary ethnology has warned against Eurocentrism, consisting of conceiving the Other as a deviation of the Same and perceiving in the infantile magma of primitive societies a still amorphous rough-hewing of our maturity. There subsists a relatively unnoticed form of ethnocentrism one could name *technocentrism*, consisting in retrospectively applying to earlier historical experiences the implicit norms of our own technology. "Communication" as it has been spoken about for almost a half-century now, its criticisms included, strongly resembles the conjunction of two extrapolations, intellectual and material: linguistics and telephonics.

Shall we be forgiven for recalling that the father of information theory, Shannon, creator of a rigorous mathematical framework for evaluating the cost of a message, was an employee of the Bell Telephone Company? This does not of course alter the scientific value of his theorems, but suggests to us the need to limit its extrapolations (to the mechanical universe). It is not a matter of indifference that in France the administration of the *Télécoms* (D.G.T., C.N.E.T., etc.) should have been the principal source of financing and sponsorship of communication studies—conferences, seminars, chaired professorships, journals and other publications. That is not to diminish their merit, nor the intense interest they generate. But such is the hold means exert over ends, and machines over minds, that an unconscious "halo effect" encourages us from those quarters to hallucinate the cultural history of human beings through the prism of the *Postes et Télécom*. A receiver, a wire, a signal. "Hello, I hear you . . . OK, received your message, good-bye." In more or less elaborate forms, this schema underlies "*the act of communication*," a central unit of its reasoning. Every scientific operation proceeds by abstraction or sampling of pertinent traits within a mass of empirical givens. So we will not fault this simplification all the more as abstract so much as *not operative*. Christianity, Protestantism, liberalisms, socialisms were not spread by wire, nor through cable, nor over radio waves. They were not telegraphic or telephonic messages. These later technologies' domestic privatization of the circulation of signs supposes a rather paltry sociability—cramped, bourgeois, or in any event, latter-day. For the most part Western history knew nothing of it, having been answerable to collective norms of transmission, more or less fusionist, whose practices of even reading itself are communitarian, and whose spoken transmission operates in a group. The priest's sermon, the schoolmaster's teaching, the grandfather's narrative, the judge's sentence addressed to a multitudinous audience, all in the bustle and murmur and surrounding ambience of a public place—church square, marketplace, princely court, hall of festivities, crossroads or calvary. Word of mouth and hearsay, which for two millennia ensured the migration of our founding myths over immense spaces, elude the theory of information and its contemporary "sub-contractings out" to other disciplines.

Clearly, the unilinear model of sender/receiver fails to apply to utterances of performative intention or calling, which we shall refer to as bound to "a built-in corporate instruction." That is, those directed or supposed to say the just and the good, that, under the common term "message," characterize the sphere of religious, social and political beliefs. Humanity's stockpile of myth was in its depths formed several thousand years ago; and moving a civilization's fabric of memory through the ages was no deed of mass media. If one turns to the history of science, the communicational model appears hardly any more pertinent, in our own "communication society," to describe the concrete modes of transmission of scientifically intended utterances.[1] Neither yesterday's doctrines nor today's bodies of knowledge seem concerned about the presuppositions of "communication."

By an odd mixture (at the beginning classical) between the tendencies to reify and to idealize, common sense implicitly treats information like an object: something that circulates in a cable between a sender and a receiver. Something that changes place, is passed around, to and fro, a little like the ball on a football field. Something that goes out from one brain to enter another, from a conceiver or a creative person to a consumer or target, for example. Common sense is not completely wrong since "information"

[1] Bruno Latour, *Science in Action: How to Follow Scientists and Engineers through Society* (Cambridge: Harvard University Press, 1987).

is also merchandise, a quantifiable raw material, a fixed-price good. But the word does not mean the same thing, in theory and in everyday life. Scientifically, information is a measurement, a statistical concept, a certain probability of occurrence and not an entity or piece of furniture. Yet this well-known *attainment* seems reduced to an *acquisition*, to the advantage of a more or less floating substantivization of the message. This latter draws its credibility at the same time from an observable reality and an immemorial habit: the signal's reality as some variation of a physical magnitude (a tension, modulation, perforation in a card, etc.) on the one hand; on the other, the tendency of our natural languages to transform all relations into an entity. But a signal, by itself, has no signification. It becomes sign only by and for a receiver. No need to recall here what all sociologists and neurobiologists know: information is not a stimulus and it does not exist in itself. We select it from among a thousand potential signals, we sort through and filter ambient stimuli according to the pertinences our cognitive aptitudes and vital needs recognize in them, we code them at the very source. The "thing to communicate" does not exist prior to and independently of the one who communicates it and the one to whom it is communicated. Sender and receiver are modified from the inside by the message they exchange, and the message itself modified by its circulation. The transmission functions as a *chain of incessant transformations* (a ball sent off round can arrive at its goal oval or even square).

We shall have other grounds, and less trivial, for challenging the notion of "act of communication" understood as a dual and punctual relation between a sending pole and receiving pole, with only a code common to the line's two extremities allowing for encoding and decoding.

Such an "act" is instantaneous. The sending (or phonation) and reception coincide in time, the agents are co-present at each end of the line. It so happens that transmission is a historical *process*, a thick temporality which is not external to but constitutive of the phenomenon, its motor and *raison d'être* (we pass on messages *in order to* do away with time, swim against the entropy, to marshall against it at the very least a "little haven of subsiding entropy").

The "act" is *interpersonal*; a performance between two, whether or not physically present to one another per se; a sequence of connected points. Yet transmission is a *collective* process. Not only are there lots of people on the "line," between the points, but in place of two individuals speaking and listening are personified social organizations, historically structured, in short, collective individuals and not isolated diodes—"silicon chips" with human faces sending each other coded signals through the ether of countless directories. The true subject of transmission is not the source of it.

The "act," in the end, is *peaceful*. It is traversed by no field of forces. But transmission is a *violent* collective process. There is conflict, sound and fury, not around or after, in the circumstances, but in the very process, informing it *from the inside*. The transmission of an idea is not ideational; a form, not formal; of a result in a science, not scientific: it puts into play all at once systems of authority and relations of domination. Every transmission is a combat, against noise, against inertia, against the other transmitters, and even—especially—against the addressees.

Christian theology was not unaware of this. The study of angels, *angelology*, which was in mythic form our first science of transmissions, is at bottom a *polemology*. "Angel" means *messenger* (*angelos*), and the angels of the Old Testament (the Good News' postal workers) are not isolated gyro-waves twirling at will. They are, like the clerics of yore, "incardinated." They are ranked in politico-military formations ("the army of Heaven," "the escort of God," etc.), under the dual sign of *antagonism* (combat against demons and the other army, Satan's) and of *hierarchy* (division into *three chairs* or army corps: seraphim, cherubim and part of the enthroned court; then dominations, virtues and powers; and finally principalities, archangels and angels). These celestial pyramids served as models for the courtly protocol and caesaro-papist ceremonial in Byzantium, which in turn served as the matrix for our monarchical (and in its wake, Republican) protocol. From Byzantine angelology came about our hierarchies of seating arrangements, our placing and order of speakers in public forums or on the editorial page, our determinations of the order of appearances in the *salon d'honneur*.

And so angels have nothing angelic about them either. Perhaps it is necessary to figure to ourselves Hermes (here may Michel Serres pardon us) as a rather wretched mediocrity. Seen in "personality profile" or by their character, those who establish schools, churches, or doctrines—in short, the colonels of effective transmission—resemble politicians more than mystics (to take up that conventional Péguyian opposition, misleading but expressive). A brief examination of the scene of contemporary ideas, including that of scientific activity, could corroborate this psychological activity, if grand history were not enough to satisfy us on this score. *No more than there is any innocent medium can there be painless transmission.* Transmission's rhyme with submission is pertinent. So too the etymology (*upakouein*, in Greek, "to listen from below, or obey").

Why? Because *to transmit is to organize*, and to organize to *hierarchize*. Hence also to exclude and subordinate—necessarily.

The decoding of signs is indeed a compound and ternary process, as Peirce emphasized; and the notion of *interpretant*, central. But what the semiologist reads behind this word, the "system of rules of translation of the message," is not what the mediologist sees there: the *instituted intermediary* charged with both closing off the message ("the complete works," "the Holy Scriptures," "the Koran," etc.) and stabilizing the interpretation by putting an end to the indefinite play of the referrals and adjournments of meanings (incompleteness demanding precisely that the area of lawful interpretations be bounded). If closure is an unattainable and always infelicitous task, incompleteness requires that the legitimate reference be established in order to "close" the group (permanence of the canonical *delimitation*). And such incompleteness automatically makes of the sender of an authorized word the simple spokesperson of a supereminent authority who is unfortunately absent (God for Jesus, Jesus for the apostle, the apostle for the Church Father, and so on, right down to the parish priest).

The formation of a *tradition of thought* is but the same thing as the formation of a *community of thought*—a collective that is the real agent of the individual communications which will subsequently take place in its wake. There is a simultaneous constituting of a *literal* corpus and an *authoritative social formation*, with its territorial closure, its idiolect, its ranks and insignia, etc. In reality, doctrine is put together retroactively by the transmitting authority that ensures for itself, through a repeated series of acts of force, the monopoly of transmission (after the canonical model of the after-effects of written religious revelations). Institution and interpretation come paired: Christian theology, for example, constructed its premises at the same time the Christian Church erected its pyramid of authorities. The transmitted form is *produced* by the corporate entity which has the authority to "close off." The "good text" is an *effect* of collective organization; if not, it will be little more than a Crusoe-like venture, a *robinsonade*. Robinson on his island unsealing the bottle fished from the sea only to find himself face to face with the encrypted message whose code he alone can make up—surely this exists only as a figment in the semiological imagination. Our "bottles" today "drift" along the course of rails, follow canalizations which owe nothing to chance, guided as they are by lines of authority. It is only in such a form that they can emerge from an ambient and deadening "noise." Those who lay out and equip the tracks or paths of passage—which are always decisive—are rarely those who sent the message on its way. The installers of the cable are most often the programmers (deciding what, out of the message produced by others, will be able to be read, seen or heard).

To the standard diagram enchaining Source-Sender-Signal-Receiver-Destination can be added one or several loops of retro-action with one or several arrows converging on the center to represent "parasites" whose provenance is the message's milieu, the source of the noise. One can, with Bateson and others, make circular this linear model; it remains nonetheless not pedagogically simplified but theoretically simplistic. This is not only because communication functions *in both directions*, the receiver being also the sender and vice versa; not only because the "noise" is essential in constituting the signal as a "good form" set against a background, which makes the "noise" primary and primordial in relation to the message. But first and foremost because transmission does not unfold or uncoil along the horizontal, between two poles situated at the same height. These poles are from the outset placed at uneven levels by an institutional relation of inequality, which is precisely what gives to the message its index of credibility. God is not at the same height as Moses, nor Moses as the Hebrew people; the Nobel prize winner in chemistry who signs an article in *Nature* is not on the same plane as the average researcher a line down (and vice versa); nor are professor and student, daughter and father: the poles go up or down, but not according to the same procedures nor the same coefficients. The "communicative event" is at best the peak limit, final surface-leveling, or compensation for an operation of transmission after its historical accomplishment. It comes *after the battle*, placing itself at the *terminus of a process it grasps by its end*—once the line has been installed, once the message has been formed as such and the code agreed by convention or institution between the partners. Communication is a transmission that has cooled, that is stable and calm. The semiological diagram (which does not question the technological standard of its era) supposes the problem resolved: the channel is installed, the hook-up done; there is someone at the other end of the line ready to listen (neither indifferent nor hostile); noise is eliminated or neutralized; and the message made credible or clearly authorized. This idyll would readily evoke scienfic communication of impersonal messages, if Bruno Latour had not already demonstrated (using the example of such and such a specialized publication) that "the scientific message is made for attack and defense: it is no more a calm place of tranquility than a bastion or bunker." [2]

If effective commercial advertisement is worth more than lengthy talk, let us open to the front page of tonight's *Le Monde*. An ad reproduces the dust jacket of the book *Catechism of the Catholic Church*, with bold print above touting "*An open book: the Church's message for taking on the Twenty-First Century*," and, below, "*A landmark and reference point, this book is an indispensable addition to every library, A DEFINITIVE TEXT.*" It is clear that the significance of the utterances announced here is not intrinsic to them and that an interpretation that would limit itself to the literal writing on the subject would miss the essential, which is its apparatus of authority. I am not alone when confronted with this text and it does not present itself by itself to my reading. It publicizes in advance and wittingly its inbuilt elevation, and the fact that it is much more than what it is: something authenticated by a community of grace (the extraordinary synod that decided on the publication, the editorial commission presided over by the *Congregatio de propaganda fide* that devised and

[2] Latour, *Science in Action*, p. 76.

developed it), all guaranteed by the highest possible ecclesiastical attestation (the Holy Father himself). We have here, taken to its strongest charismatic power, a procedure of accreditation that, in an (infinitely) lesser measure, affects a number of texts a reader meets with nowadays: traversed by an aura, carried across by an authority (instituted or informal), stage-directed by a formal presentation, fitted out with a prior *system of instructions*, that we will call the *meta-text*. The transmission of even the most secular and positive documents does not depart from these rules. Let us take Michel Foucault's *Orders of Discourse*. Its lettered literality does not present itself bare to the decodings of my inspection. Bearing the hallmark of its editor, the solemnity of its circumstances, the reviews of the scholarly press, the flattering rumor that has borne it all the way to me, it is indexed from the start as a *value* that valorizes. To make its content my own, is to include myself, needless to say only fantastically, among the intellectual and social elite that heard it delivered *in vivo*, *in situ*, in a prestigious institution; it is to purloin its repertory, learn its passwords. The social signified of an utterance is the group, real or imaginary, for which it serves as reference. Hence a reading by private conscience alone becomes by ricochet communitarian—becomes the surreptitious appeal to a posthumous co-optation or discreet entry into a fantasmatic and enviable orchestra, that of readers more or less complicit that the author has directed or led during his or her lifetime, and continues in our thoughts to animate from beyond the grave.

2. Mediology Generation

Transmission is thus not communication. As to semiology, let us avow from the very outset without shame or vanity our willed immunity to it. More than an acknowledgment arising out of temperament, this is a reasoned choice. Its range extends far. One will not get anywhere in the intelligence of symbolic traditions, it seems to us, without breaking these moorings. Without parting with the elder "epistemological break" of the code, our main obstacle. The mediological conversion proves to be at this price.

Does science take an S-shaped course? Like God, does the

knowledge of man write up and down with curved lines? After the "linguistic turn" of the century's beginning (the *Course in General Linguistics* was published in 1916), the mediological turn initiated and announced by multiple researchers sets off in the other direction along a gradual curve. Taking the first bend, we had willingly left things and events behind, to rediscover the autonomy of signifying organizations and practices in the form of systems of internal relations. Dissipating the *referential illusion* was a true liberation. This formalization made it possible to have done with empiricism and the psychological incantation. The turn that is gradually taking shape under our footsteps leads toward being free from the *semiotic illusion*, in order to again find a strong reference to the world, its materials, its vectors and its procedures. And this will again be a liberation.

The subject of studies that has been baptized S.I.C. (Sciences of Information and Communication) in our universities could not help yielding importance to the Signsong; and cannot now *not* help topping it. "Semio" had a good half-decade's start on "medio." And that was fair enough. Structural linguistics having come first in the chronology of formalizations, it served as a basis for unifying neighboring and competing human sciences. "The battle for the code was a battle against the ineffable" (Eco). It was a Thirty Years War fortunately won: having remained schoolmistress of the field and campuses, semiology has reigned ever since then in the same pedagogical spaces that once excluded it, but by self-replication, self-citation and self-reference. The one-time heretics of the university since that time now embody its orthodoxy. And so the new positivities signal a change of season, climate and paradigm. And to say "the moderns have become the ancients," "semiology is behind us," is not to evade but take up the work of funeral arrangements and mourning. Killing the father in France has never hurt the chrysanthemum business. Emancipated but in no ways acting like ingrates, mediologists will go to pay their respects over Saussure's tomb like proper prodigal sons, and will keep prominently displayed on their mantlepiece photos of his two most brilliant European nephews on the language side: Roland Barthes and Umberto Eco. Without them, the meeting of the telephonic receiver and phonologic combinatory (christened "semiology of communication") would never have acquired such notoriety.

Does it need pointing out that we are not propounding the return to the subject, like the orphaned souls of the time of structuralist logics, no more than we are proclaiming the rights of content over form? Along with others, we propose the opposite: going to the object (and thereby finding the subject again in its historical and overt concreteness); going resolutely to the "machinistic," to "technico-instrumental rationality," to the "technician's system" and other pejorative terms; going, therefore, in a contrary direction from Habermas, Adorno, or Ellul. This amounts to giving precedence to the material base on which cultures rest. Even if the contribution of a theological component seems to us to need figuring into the objects of inquiry—as a "primordial soup" of anthropology—it is a matter of pursuing rationalization where it is headed, by shaking off the last magical subjections. Our place is, then, in the ranks with those who "advocate the letter against the spirit, extension (in space) versus comprehension, space against duration, surface against content," to take up the terms Canguilhem uses to characterize the works of François Dagognet. Those watchwords are drily anatomical indeed, for the philosopher, ascetic. Morphological, descriptive, externalizing, uncertain with Valéry that things even have depth of content—the mediological sensibility chafes at going to the bottom of things, keeping to "the faces, surfaces and interfaces" of things. We would like to make this recommendation our own: "A modern artist (a scientist?) must spend two thirds of his time trying to see what is visible and above all not seeing what is invisible. Philosophers expiate often enough the mistake of directing their efforts toward the very opposite." Two-thirds for the less than ordinary, one-third for the super-sensory: the proportion seems judicious. Is it not the same distribution of wakefulness to sleep?

Within the ordinariness of the everyday, we would like then to join with those who apprehend the interior by the exterior, resolutely drawing each *idea* toward the *realia* that support or bear it along. In the case at hand: this means drawing the *sign* toward the *trace*, *discourse* uttered toward *distance* covered [*parcours*], *interpretation* toward *instrumentation*, *text* toward *document*, *writing* toward *inscription*, *communication* itself toward *the paths of communication* (routes, canals or channels, railroads), *orality* toward *vocality*, *memory* toward *memories*—or the material media for recording traces, with the technological *mnemonics* or procedures of coding and storage associated with them (literal, analogical, numerical, etc.). To take each ideal essence back to the practical operation that makes it exist has nothing novel about it, but by no means goes without saying as far as "the life of the mind" is concerned, so naturally is this domain inclined (by the bias of our Indo-European languages, notably) to a substantive and idealizing approach. Needless to say, perceptible data will not suffice for these exercises of translation. The procedure of transmission needs to be reconstructed anew on each occasion: the "self-erasing" (Bougnoux) nature of the medium does not render it easily graspable. Bringing the materialities of culture to light in their mutual relations supposes a methodical apprenticeship of the unseen evidence: hyperphenomenalism is not an empiricism.

3. Retrospective Glance

The history of the "Saussure years" in French culture has already been traced, and very skillfully. Or we should say the "Lévi-Strauss years"—if we kept to the positive gains of this period and if the double passion or double knowledge of artistic and natural phenomena had not personally protected the great anthropologist against the errancy of the pan-logician. Birth of the hero, fabulous friendships, tournaments of champions, Ulyssean wonderings and philosopher stones: whatever taste one might have for the Christian or Structuralist marvelous, we will not recount here this collective *chanson de geste* presumed already known.[3] Let our analysis be limited to the constituent of "communication" for a reminder of the sources.

It is known that by de-historicizing linguistics in order to align it with the notion of *system*, Ferdinand de Saussure made it into a science at the beginning of the century. He expounded it as part of a general science to come, "that studies the life of signs at the center of social life," itself "part of social psychology," to which he gave the name *semiology*. It was this, a few decades later, that

---

[3] François Dosse, *Histoire du structuralisme*, tome I (*Le Champ du signe*) (Paris: La Découverte, 1991).

Roland Barthes raised into a magnetic north pole of the human sciences, under the name of "general semiology." The latter's articulations, looking no longer toward a social psychology passed over in silence, were supposed to fall under "a quadrivium of pilot sciences"—economy, linguistics, ethnology and history. Bearer of this good news, the appearance of *Elements of Semiology* in 1964 combined the contributions of Saussure (the language/word, signifier/signified, syntagm/system couplings) and those of Hjelmslev (the schema/norm/usage trilogy). Semiology is presented here as a subgroup of structural linguistics. Holding it better to bring disciplines still in formation in line with an already formalized body of knowledge than the converse, the genealogical table-turning was only fair. Linguists who scarcely recognized in semiology their own offspring protested in vain against these hasty expropriations. No matter how much the transfer of one mode of thought into other domains of competence may have led to excesses, it takes its place in the development of ideas, repeating the pattern as the dominant structures of learning have seen fit. (The observation applies also to the mediologist, sensitive in particular to the *ecological* model of intelligibility.)

Barthes' text was published in the review *Communications*, founded in 1960. In the name of this master word there took place at that time the symbiosis between an empiricist sociology of the means of symbolic diffusion and circulation, in the American mode, and a theoretical semiology that was pointed and specialized in the European mode.

1950–1980: the boom in semiotic cults sees itself stimulated by the concomitant one in "mass culture." The first superstition serving as receiving structure for the second. It hardly seemed important that the linguistic "grid" was also a protective screen, diverting researchers from taking a deeper look at the new practices and devices from within a historical continuum that had found its start in the Neolithic (as Leroi-Gourhan was doing at the same moment, in great isolation, with *Gesture and Speech*). On the surface the concomitance seemed providential. On one side, the development of mass communications was enlarging the field of meaning or signification; on the other, the theoreticians of the code were enlarging their field of interpretation: mass culture was no longer vulgar, the academic discipline no longer elitist.

Semiology's love for Publicus crossed with the semiologist's love for Panzani pasta publicity, unbeknownst to the protagonists, knotting together in unexpected reciprocity a popularity and a sophistication. At a moment when philosophical work was splitting from the interests of the everyday, and when belles lettres were disappearing from the social horizon, the theme of communication was re-opening all sorts of passages between academic abstraction and the most vibrant modernity. The review *Communications* was then one of the hot spots for the short circuits opened between Saussure and James Bond, or Hjemslev and Hitchcock, a seductive compression with, alas, uncertain scientific fallout.

Without passing through linguistics at all, Norbert Wiener (inventor of cybernetics) had already as early as 1948 defined man without reference to interiority as a communication machine, a machine for exchanging information with his environment. The idea that all reality must be broken up in the final analysis into a set of relations between elements came together by an entirely different angle with the structural postulate, imputing every effect of meaning to a combination of minimal units or pertinent traits of a determinate code. While resolutely unaware of it, French semiology was metaphorizing and "culturalizing" the American mechanist paradigm. From the domains of metaphor to immediate surroundings, all aspects of social life soon came under the empire of signs. "Culture," as Umberto Eco was to sum it up soon after, "is essentially communication," that is, "emitting messages subordinated to underlying codes." Why? Because all phenomena of culture are systems of signs, a sign being something (no matter what) "through whose knowledge we become familiar with something other," according to Peirce's definition. Sign systems overflow, in extension; linguistic phenomena but obey, in intention, the same rules of construction. The codes of communication subsume the sphere of natural languages—which do not definitively stabilize the model since they are themselves modeled by the "code" structure. One will be able to transpose the "system of communication" to the analysis of the unconscious ("structured like a language"), of Gothic architecture, of the fashions of dress, of the filmic image, of painting, of advertising posters, and thus to infinity. Logocentrism can swallow everything. The problem comes from what it assimilates. Relieving the concepts of linguistics from the constraints that gave them meaning and from the field that witnessed their birth, this imperialism of youth caused a slippage from the hypothetical model of explication to the ontological categorization of the object in need of explanation. Its triumph would make it possible, again in Umberto Eco's words, to "reduce the facts of nature to phenomena of culture," or more still to "translate nature into society and culture."[4] Thus by the fiction of codes conceived as "structural models of *possible* communicative exchange" one could reduce here and there what Lacan was calling at the same moment "realist imbecility." Pasolini himself was not exempt from this latter when he saw the filmic image as an *analogon* of reality, the reproduction on screen of a preexisting object (André Bazin had possessed the same enthusiasm for the rendered miraculousness of life). In fact, in Eco's correction, film is a code of conventional signs proper to our culture, "a language that speaks another pre-existing language."[5]

Man dwells in language and there is no before-language. It founds everything, and itself (as following Heidegger, "poetic speech explains things but nothing can explain poetic speech nor speech [*la parole*] in general"). The expulsion of the referent that inheres in these types of combinatories closes off the language onto itself—and into a self-referential dizziness which led Saussure, in his day, on a hunt through religious esoterism and spiritist seances for a code of codes as the ultimate foundation. Others, more circumspect, stick to that polite form of aesthetically rich, provocative and often evocative schizophrenia that the recycling of absolute idealism engenders in the commentary of actuality. Maintaining that "denotation is never anything but the most beautiful and subtle of connotations" (put clearly, that everything is an effect of style), the excellent author of *For a Critique of the Political Economy of the Sign*, for example, stays faithful to this premise when he concludes that the Gulf War never happened. It is a coherent and even rigorous point of view.

---

[4] Umberto Eco, *La Structure absente: Introduction à la recherche sémiotique* (Paris: Le Mercure de France, 1972), pp. 222 and 224.
[5] Ibid., p. 224.

For what mysterious reason?

> Master Mind on its man perched
> Kept in its folds its mystery . . .
> I've forgotten the rest.

This apologue by Valéry, that great precursor-mediologist—it is one of his *Mean and Other Thoughts*—had long range. "The rest" recalls itself every day to our attention. Daniel Bougnoux observed that "One always thinks emergently and off the very top of the pile, and what is 'well known' is as a matter of fact *not* recognized or fully processed mentally. Each emergent level reorganizes everything under its own law, and fails to understand or misreads in this measure the lower levels which, for all that, do not cease to support it." Such would indeed be the moral of Valéry's fable, and the intellectualist origin of the semiotic "hubris" and immoderacy. The cavalier top-of-the-heap-only view of things has abracadabrized away the material level of meaning—and for having too fully deciphered the world as sign, we forget there is a world underneath, and that the letter itself has a body. We do not bother to measure the deep layers of orality out of which print culture historically proceeds when we are fully submerged in print culture; nor does the urbanite remember the sky, water torrents and paths, and the universe of the senses, of the sensory experience of smell, taste and touch. No more than this does the sign recollect the thing and itself as trace. Mallarmé: "To meditate on something and leave no traces becomes evanescent." But when there *is* a trace—ink and paper—it also fades from the view of the person who meditates on his or her meditations, just as the celluloid and the camera disappear in the projected film.

The paradox we face is that of having to begin from the all-semantic in order to rediscover after the fact the technical means, the gesture and the material base that are all so *well* known, and thus unknown—and that brought the all-semantic onto the scene in the first place.

The empire of signs is that of megalopolises (like the Japanese conurbation), and the planet's global-villageification and citification have ordered and legitimized the transformation of things into "signs," including pictures and images. We produce meaning with our codes, yes, but starting from a physical experiential fact. The photograph for instance, "a sign actually affected by the object" and a raw fragment-affect, takes hold of us as the absoluteness of a presence independent of our mental representations and social conventions. And this grabbing hold lessens within us the grip of codes, at least for a short instant. An oil painting too has its brushwork, its texture, its thickness more or less tactile. Lévi-Strauss, hardly under suspicion for empiricism and writing about abstract music itself (the space par excellence of arbitrariness and code, with its sound system not at all prescribed by nature), not long ago recalled that "in the same respect as painting, [it] presupposes a natural organization of sense experience, which is not the same thing as saying it undergoes it itself." It is noteworthy that the Lévi-Straussian oeuvre, whose debt to Jakobson and structural phonology as well as to empirical investigation is well known, should have always set itself apart from the approaches of its formalist neighbors in terms of a particular "deference toward objects and technologies." Seeing how our more casuistical linguistic contortions have pulled off the fine double of getting rid of the tools at the same time as the bodies, technology and the sensorium having vanished together, one can regret that our best semiologists have not paid more attention to this passage from the inaugural address of the chair of social anthropology given by Lévi-Strauss at the Collège de France (1960):

> In positing the symbolic nature of its object, social anthropology does not intend to cut itself off from *realia*. How could it, when art, in which all is sign, utilizes material media? One cannot study gods while ignoring their images; rites without analyzing the objects and substances manufactured and manipulated by the officiant; or social rules independently of the things that correspond to them. Social anthropology . . . does not separate material culture and spiritual culture.[6]

---

[6] Claude Lévi-Strauss, *Structural Anthropology*, vol. II, tr. Monique Layton (New York: Basic Books, 1976), p. 11.

Basically our minor, localized bid or analytical assault on symbolic power keeps to the straight and narrow of this general
recommendation. It is not a matter of indifference, in any event,
that the putative father or at least great-uncle of the semiological
generation should have been the first, while offering this advice
to all and no one in particular, to put his finger on the very
weakest point.

4. The Magic of Intelligence

Semiotic consciousness often recalls the "primitive mentality"
observed by Lévy-Bruhl. It has something intoxicating, like
magic. Not only because it sees signs everywhere, the way witches
and those with second sight do, but because it thinks it can interpret them against its own backgrounds, "internally." If man *is*
language and if everything around him is as well, we no longer
see any need to discover, become an exile, equip oneself. The
human mind can know the world external to it while remaining
with or next to itself (in a Hegelian "never-far-from-oneself" [*bei
sich*]). To this metaphysical advantage is added more specialized
gratifications in the intellectual's case that should hardly astonish
the mediologist. Within a given social milieu, a message reaches
epidemic proportions when it guarantees that milieu's vital interests. To inform all those who can and do engage in speech by
profession (universities, publishing houses, newspapers, etc.) that
it is better to busy oneself with words than things; and to inform
all those people of learning in general that all facts of society and
nature must, if they are to be understood, be translated into
deeds of culture—this does not leave one exposed to being
rebuffed by those to whom the message is addressed. The Mind's
narcissism is the corporate penchant of intellectuals. When it is
the utterances that suit us best that are appropriated the fastest,
professionals who talk for a living (and especially the psycholo-
gists who stake their reputation, practice and revenues in and
through language) do not turn a deaf ear. Nothing could better
establish analysis by right and in fact than the *structural ade-
quation of the object to the tool* ("the unconscious is structured
like a language"). "One psychoanalyzes only adults who know

how to speak" (Diatkin), and this will be practiced all the better given the postulate—contradicting the most flagrant observable facts—that "the child is caught up in language from birth," and that the natural biological substratum Freud constantly refers to must first be recoded in Saussurian terms (Freud, afflicted with his "naive physicalism," not having properly understood psychoanalysis). A tempting dream, this: to produce the metalanguage of all languages, and re-beget every event by producing its law of begetting. The world is garbled speech, but I who know its codes shall give it back transparence. The *"meta"* level becomes the one that transforms into "objects," and thus into lower-stage, all the other levels. Whoever accedes to it is transformed into a cultural Grand Subject. Since this novel, this thriller, this poem declines (as one possible version among many others) into a generative model whose keys I possess, I become its master at a critical distance, at the very least its equal in inventiveness. The encoding on all fronts of the manifestations of human genius—with the translations and passings it authorizes from one to the other—places the Decoder at the upper reaches of the sources of meaning and makes him into the author of authors, a creator to the second power. To "semiotize" a text, a film, a commercial poster, a program is in some sense to turn them into satellites. The critic turns sunlike, pulling works and products one by one from his deconstructable discourse as if out of a hat containing a thousand secrets. We are by now familiar with the social conjurer's tricks that this dazzling posturing of superiority earned for Lacan.[*]

A veneer of semiology confers intelligence by limiting the expense, far from adherence to the cause or the exertions of more conventionally professional practice. This remoteness can serve to win over the most malicious (those unaware that it is often necessary to push intelligence to the point where one dares to be foolish), and one could set "medio" against "semio" as one might set humor against irony. For the ruminants of culture that we are, to say the least, so used to chewing the cud of the printed page in

---

[*]For a *chronique intime* of the man (and era) to whom Debray alludes, readers might wish to consult Elisabeth Roudinesco's *Jacques Lacan & Co.: A History of Psychoanalysis in France, 1925–1985,* tr. Jeffrey Mehlman (Chicago: University of Chicago Press, 1990). [Trs.]

all its humbling pedestrian literalism, semiology loomed overhead like our vault of heaven. It made it possible for us to look up
from grazing, and yet this without leaving our philological pen,
our "informational stockade." It was as if the relief of a broader
vista had finally been sanctioned, granting to the more creative
imaginers of the symbolic order this paradox: an apparent change
of locale in the very midst of the most familiar surroundings.

Saint Thomas and his *summa* did not educate in vain the
young medievalist Umberto Eco in the deductions of formal
logic. Like every good scholastic, general semiology is a didactics.
For epigones, this easily memorized grid of plotted functions
makes it possible to speak plausibly of all things with the help of
a dozen or so diads (denotation/connotation, message switching
or commutation/permutation, Language/Speech, etc.). When you
are stepping out to dine this evening, don't leave home without
Paradigm and Syntagm. Your companion's attire, the restau-
rant's menu, the dining room's interior decoration, and the check:
their eloquence is yours without risk of any silly remarks. If
indeed "the formalization everywhere at work optimizes communication between men," the one "explaining" the other, this
commonly accepted holy writ is the optimum of the theoreticians
of communication; and its terminology, adopted as the general
equivalent of the patchy and laborious knowable things it dispenses us from acquiring, becomes what would otherwise be the
small change of the artisanal masteries one can now afford to disdain. With the transactions of semiotic recognition conducted in
a reflexive and reflective way, *en miroir*, "a semiology seminar"
is almost a redundance, the semiotician a born colloquist, and an
isolated semiologist a contradiction in terms (whence this advice
to researchers: to make friends and influence people learn tennis
and semiotics). A direct effect of metalanguage (or language as
metamodel), being global and englobing by nature, is to render
discussion interdisciplinary and international. It is not enough
that the best solutions be "local, singular, specific, suited to circumstance, original" (Michel Serres); they are also, and indeed
owing to this very character, painful to find. But it is not required
that one learn architecture, be familiar with painting, cooking,
fashion, commercial advertising or film, with the procedures and
vocabulary proper to each of these competencies, in order to

speak well about them semiologically. Taking the externals of each activity for its internality, the arts and trades hygenically cleansed of what is unique to their technical practice—this economical discipline allows neat and elegant demonstrations by arranging and classing the most varied materials under a single "proper form." This advantage also has its drawbacks. And one is always a little amazed to hear pedagogues complain about the difficulties students fresh from their schooling have with moving on to actually *doing* something: writing a screenplay, making a low-budget amateur film, building a shed, composing some statement about love or taxes. That they should encounter confusion in such applications may not be unrelated to the false rigor of presuppositions they bring to them.

"It is when the thing itself is absent that we have to put the sign in its place," Ferrante observes in *The Dead Queen*. If for the man of words the thing itself goes by the name of style, talent, or sensibility, then the Sign's heralds were well supplied with it. But by this logic, whenever it is there, in their work, their knowledge of it [*science*] no longer is, and vice versa. As if the stylist and the-oretician had going a game of hide-and-seek. There is always a danger when pitting intellectual discovery against academic tact and flexibility, the inventors against the doctors. This venerable contestation is all too easy; and we lack the means to play the prosecutors. Who wouldn't like to have the literary talent of the master-practitioners of the Textual? A tree is judged by its fruits, and the semiological apple branch has produced its share of delectables. Barthes made a true writer's *oeuvre* out of criticism. And a comely come-on, *The Name of the Rose*, became a masterpiece. How can one ward off the impression that the savoriness of the creative or fictional impulse in such works laughs at its counter, learnedness? Or that this emotion or this verve, this subtle tristfulness or this *gaya scienza* (depending on whether one reads Barthes or listens to Eco) owes so little to *esprit de système*. It does happen that rhetoricians can be better than their rhetoric. Here intuitions exceed method. *Fragments of a Lover's Discourse* or *Camera Lucida* do not seem really to draw from the same wellsprings as the *Elements of Semiology* or *The System of Fashion*. As if whatever depth was contained in the aesthete's humours came to underscore what was superficial in the rigor of the "scientist." It is besides this no slight paradox that these enemies of the ineffable and emotion owed their brightest prestige, as it turned out, to *literary* ineffableness and emotion. This gentle putting-right or subversion of the writer as a producer in process, an *écrivant*, by the more traditional writer as author, *écrivain*, marks perhaps indeed the extreme of elegance, the height of tact and irony. Still another contemporary "structuralist" would be found to have pushed this discrepancy to its limits of madness. "Louis" was a greater genius than Althusser. He died at the breaking point between these two extremes. What possible likeness exists between *Reading "Capital"* and *The Future Lasts Forever* or *Journal of Captivity*? In the case of his Marxist side as well, the musician buried the professor, de-sanctioning his theory with a gesture of posthumous derision, all the more cruel because involuntary. But let's call time out from paying all these respects. The mere existence of saints, heroes and geniuses who stand out from the rest still does not signify that they should be intellectually right to think what they think and not something else. The exceptional personalities we have run across in the course of our life and who fully lived up to one or another of these glowing terms—among men of action, of forms or of thought—were generally speaking (and hard though it be for us to admit) more given over to delusion than to being in the right. Reason, alas, must have something of the reasonable about it. Its preferences go to the mediocre. And so mediology will do without geniuses. Its very dull grayness itself is, as it stands, something for which it should be given credit.

5. On a Few Handicaps

In January 1969 in Paris, the international steering committee of the International Association of Semiotics adopted a resolution of the utmost importance: to trade in the term "semiology" for "semiotics." A mere influence from English, one might remark. Yes, but also and above all a political decision. The suffix -*ics* is an authority-amplifier. It hardens the soft human-science non-scientificity and modernizes the old. Thus the consonantal rhyme with computronics, telematics, robotics, the electronics of home automation [*domotique*]. The semiotician is a technician or specialized mechanic. The mediologist is an ideologue. The *-ics*: clear-cut suffix of the exact. The *-logy*: a liquid suffix of the approximate. Where the *-ics* will at least fix a figurative breakdown by positing a code, the *-logy* is all talk and only talk. That's the difference of their status. But dare we suggest that the rhyming *-ics* can be misleading? One can after all give a hard appearance to soft idealities, and by the same token, softly analyze realities that are hard (obstructive, angular, vexatious).

It matters little if mediology just manages to eke out a living, without any fixed domicile: the important thing is that it gets some exercise. Doubtless in science as in art, the home institution's word is law. It is the *docere*, the official instruction, that makes doctrine, and not the other way round: the domiciliation of discourse is its first accreditation. Far from us, therefore, is the idea of being able to somehow one day compete with the semiotic canon fortified by its teaching corps, impressive international network of endowed chairs and reviews, conferences, symposia, associations, research centers, etc. Our course of inquiry has indeed taught us that it is precisely corporate organizations which think, and not minds. This accounts for the consideration we bring to these intellectual administrations, more resistant than a Party or an International. They have asked so much effort of the founders and provide so many benefits to the followers that they end up reproducing themselves. It's the norm: *homo sapiens* is an animal of habits, *homo academicus* even more so.

A political science of mind, spirit, or collective consciousness [*l'esprit*], if it were to take shape, would not moreover have anything to offer in which professional thinkers might take pleasure. It was after all the disdain for meaning's viscosities and dullnesses or inertia that made semiology take wing among the literary population. To bring up the technological, economical and political underside of signs means offering those who study the crafting of meanings the proposition of a real depreciation, making them lose by comparison. Our present observations, unpleasant and misplaced, are themselves proof of this (it takes a doggedly foolish reductivism to remove an intellectual's debate toward a vulgar territory of positions, alliances and networks by nature foreign to men of learning). The mediologist's *meta* is the semiologist's *infra*. Whatever intelligibility the first will earn, he will lose in respectability. In the same measure that analysis of our *myths* flatters the professionals of the word, the observation of our tools puts them off.

In our ethnographic labors concentrating on various given populations of signs, we would like to have drawn from the meticulous material descriptions of the paleontologist. André Leroi-Gourhan (who produced no literary work) is not a very frequently cited author, his reputation not having passed beyond specialized circles. It seems to us however that the luminous figure of the prehistorian he represented sheds more light on our modernity (including political and social modernity) even if his erudite oeuvre holds a more than modest place in the French "intellectual landscape" (judging by the map of cultural journalism). The living development of the species as of the individual closely combines brain and hand, the symbolic mastery of external habitat and the physical-chemical exploitation of matter. The hand and the face, technology and language, have unfortunately not received the same public and scientific consideration, particularly in the recent period. Yet truly "tool-and language-using are bound together neurologically, and the one and the other are inseparable in the social structure of humanity" (Leroi-Gourhan, *Gesture and Speech*). Exclusive insistence on language has transformed the sciences of man into the sciences of a half-man, something comparable to a person missing one leg or with one hemisphere amputated from the brain. In France within our human sciences the name of Leroi-Gourhan can be associated with the one, and that of Lévi-Strauss with the other, of the two antinomic and complementary poles of anthropology. If we were to be able in however small a way to draw out from the shadows—along with many others more qualified than we are (I am thinking here especially of Simondon and Stiegler)—and succeed in highlighting *the archeological and technological side of the world of symbolic representations* (which is the portion of that world traditionally considered accursed), we would feel that justice as much as truth would have been served.

Through its linguistic guidance, semiology constructs system and theorem. Through *its* openness to technological fact, a mediology can only frame problems and conduct research. It is, obviously, not a doctrine, but a *sphere of influence*, a *framework of study*, a *field of research*.

Like any systematic architecture, a semiotics that "examines each sign system in relation to the laws of language" (Eco) possesses not only an object but a method which can be expounded by *deduction* from an a priori model, in this case the model of structural linguistics. The rule here precedes the case.

A transdisciplinary intersection, mediology proceeds a posteriori by *induction*, starting from a bundle of historical inquiries. The cases, here, precede the rule.

Each one of these procedures has its known disadvantages.

A deductive system produces logical sequences, but ones that when seen up close can be shown to be inexact and objectless (for example: the reasoning that the universe in general and images in particular are decipherable like a text). An inductive discipline produces *results*, but ones that are not easily formalized.

One cannot widen one's field of investigation without losing something of formal rigor. Formalization goes hand in hand with closure. By deliberately boxing itself into the taxonomic formalities of the code, semiology won marks for its external signs of "scientificity." But the abstraction became in the long run a tight grip that would not loosen, and only a new opening up could relieve it of this formalist cramp. In this sense "semio" and "medio" cannot see eye to eye. The second one does not demote the first but recreate it, as one star in a disciplinary constellation.

What seems questionable is not the validity of semiotic discourse in its own province, but its inflation. From being an invitation to adventure, semiology has followed, in the wake of narrative, filmic, kinesic (gestural), gastronomical, etc., semiotics, the degrading path toward becoming a way of administering a kind of no-fault insurance. A frequent trajectory for a locally pertinent system: earn range by earning credit, but devalue oneself finally into a universal can opener. But by the same token, when the day comes that in college literature classes decoding Madame de Sévigné's letters will have yielded the forefront to the study of postal relays between Grignan and Paris, of the goose quill pens used by this letter-writer and the mills where her stationery was manufactured, the mediologist would be wise to reach for the alarm bell . . . But that day is thankfully far off.

6. Interpreting and Organizing:
To Each his Vocation

"Be on your guard, André Breton, not to figure later on in the literary history textbooks; while if *we* set our sights on honor, it would be inscription for all posterity in the history of cataclysms." The young Daumal who heckled in this manner the pope of the Surrealists, in 1930, did not evidently succeed in joining the ranks of Genghis Khan, Hitler or Stalin. The mediologist hasn't the poet's presumption. But it is definitely the history of cataclysms that circumscribes his horizon, not the history of literature. The warmongers do not interest him any less than the good authors. So too with how one transits from the one to the other.

Crowning literary studies, semiotic decrypting proposes soft technologies, in which one processes and exhausts one's object, the meaning of a text, by means of another text: information here oscillates within the spectrum of very low energies belonging to the physics of the displacements of meaning. When Umberto Eco was disturbed to see his essay *The Open Work* (1962) give legitimacy to certain transports of interpretation and takes it upon himself to temper the fanaticism of his partisans (*The Limits of Interpretation*, Paris, in 1992), it is in order to defend the rights of the original, restore the preeminence of the letter (as the normative parameter of possible readings). There are some things that are just *givens*, he reminds us, and we cannot infinitely deconstruct as the whim takes us. But "given" here meaning "text," the last word will remain at the words themselves. When it comes to the mediologist, he defends the right of the text—a text that is born from experiences and needs unfamiliar to the order of words—*to produce something other than text*. Or rather: because ever since the invention of printing men have mixed symbolic information with political decision-making, battles of interpretation with battles plain and simple involving real casualties and real arms (as in the iconoclasts' quarrel of images, the wars of religion or nationalistic insurrections), the mediologist would like to follow close-up the *extra-logical avatars of the logos*. And because an instance of *saying*, under certain conditions, can produce a *doing*, or a *having (causing) something (to be) done* (something different from a book having some bearing on an older book). He breaks the philological yoke, for violence is in the history of discourses themselves (committing the historiographer to frequenting rather dubious or shady circles, including those of princes, warrior-monks, and rascals).

In spilling over systematically onto what is outside the text (like an off-piste skier), the mediologist does not just tack on a wee bit of "pragmatism" (by which we understand the study of relations between signs and their senders or interpreters) to lots of "textualism." His intention is not to enrich or perfect extant semiology with a sprig of cultural or political sociology, cobbling together in the universe of ideas the equivalent of what the aesthetics of reception has been able to bring to the universe of forms. He must not only complicate but overturn the order of factors. Put the Church *before* the Gospel, the Party *before* the theory, the School before the Textbook. The orchestra before the musical score.

There is not here any "unacceptable reading" since the question of intentionality behind the work or of the author is no longer what keeps the door of meaning propped open. "If Jack the Ripper were to come say to us his acts were guided by inspiration received reading the Gospel," writes Umberto Eco, "we would be inclined to think he read the New Testament in an unusual way."[7] This diet of the unusual is our daily bread. Where the semiologist says "betrayal!" the mediologist says "transmission." "*Traduttore, traditore*"—all translation is treason—is law. Not that the *reader*'s intention necessarily takes precedence over the work's; but the subjective perversion of the interpreter counts less than the objective logic that assigns to every organized collection or whole, to every stable community, the constraint of a text or a myth of founding. And its "interpretation" will be, then, the effect (just like the text itself in its sovereign unity) of a programmed sequence of organizing acts, in such a way that it is the organizational use of a cited text that calls for a certain type of reading, and not the reverse. The pragmatics of usages determines the semiotics of codes. The French Revolution invented "the Enlightenment" (as a meaningful rallying around a cause), and the Catholic magisterium invented (one century after Jesus) the New

---

[7] Umberto Eco, *The Limits of Interpretation* (Bloomington: Indiana University Press, 1990), p. 83.

Testament. The womb comes *after* the child, who shapes it in his own measure. The words of the prophet are put in his mouth posthumously. all this according to the law of the precursor, "the one of whom one knows afterward that he came before."

Contrasting Derrida's position with that of Marie Bonaparte toward Edgar Allan Poe's "Purloined Letter," Eco distinguishes between *interpretation*, which stands by the text as a given, and *utilization*, when we claim to draw out of the text inferences about its author's person. The observation of historical facts shows that the social use or the actual career of reception of a text exceeds the alternative of persons and statements. It demonstrates first of all that its users are not reduced to readers, and still less to exegetes. From a plus side, Jack the Ripper, like Gregory VII or Torquemada, were as legitimate interpreters of the New Testament as Stalin or Pol Pot were of *Das Kapital*, because the mediologist is under no obligation to ask himself questions about legitimacy. He acknowledges that every strategy of interpretation is subordinate to a strategy of appropriation: it is a political operation, and thus an exclusion. Property in this case *is* theft: letters that are useful are always "stolen." The problem is not that of interpreting properly or badly the parable of the Good Samaritan or the analysis of labor-value, it is knowing how to make use of it to keep one's appointment in charge of department x or advising director y. One can in extreme cases use an author without knowing him, just as one undergoes the influence of a text without having read a line of it. That is even the most frequent case. How many of those who lived in the Communist world had read Karl Marx in his textual form? Or in the medieval world, Aristotle and Saint Thomas? Or from our politically liberal world, Adam Smith or Montesquieu? How many, even today, subjects of the Freudian empire have read the works of Freud? The projected cone of a collection of utterances passes beyond the immediate space of its "addressees," whether followers or victims. It sows its seeds indirectly, off to the side, in a "pre-recorded" and re-broadcast sort of way, through a thousand roundabout pathways. And most often its memory precedes it. Those endowed with farsightedness it reaches mediated by rumor, indeed magnified by its opacity and its exegetical escorts, as if basking in the glow of these thousand silent signs, non-verbal and unwritten—in the manner of rituals, buildings, emblems honoring the (real or supposed) author of the primordial text. To acquire such a text, look at and thumb through it: this is to come back into the exaltedly fulfilling community of those who speak in its name. Whether religious or doctrinal, the most highly valued Books of the societies of the book have this status—that possessed by the Koran of today's Islam. The *meta-text*—or that collection of indications of the relation which propriety demands one maintain toward it—envelops the text and causes it to exist socially.

And so we are dealing with a turning around of the usual signposts. The semiologist relates a given text to its past, the mediologist to its future. "Have I really understood?" asks the one. "Where is this going to end up?" asks the other? The interpreter is tormented by the "what-can-one-*say*-about-it?" The speaker-participant, by the "what-can-one-*make*-of-it?" There is a characteristic semiological personality—ironical, uninvolved, nonviolent, skeptical, relativistic, or of sunny disposition—whose traits alone bespeak professional competence and *habitus*. Semiologists are not active in politics, even when and especially when having come out of a more scientific horizon they make themselves into hermeneuts of everyday life, like Eco the chronicler and Barthes the mythologist. The psychological profile of the mediologist is perhaps less contemplative, closer to collective action. But for a wild enthusiasm for grandeur, he is a strategist manqué or suppressed poltico. At the least he loved once upon a time the battlefields. *Mutatis mutandis*, semiological flair is distinguished from mediological instinct, like the detective from the (disarmed) prophet. In the one case one's eye is on Sherlock Holmes, in the other on Saint Paul. These two individuals can cross paths in the street, and chat for a spell, since it takes all sorts to make a world. But they do not have, the one and the other, the same obligations. One can see that in order to be complementary, semiology and mediology do not answer to the same vital interests.

7. "Medium is Message": A Critique's Critique

Was McLuhan's name too often in the newspapers for him to be taken seriously by the academy? The proper name's transfiguration into logo, trademark and cliche (a match in acoustic space to the

Marlboro man, Chaplin's cane or Marilyn's flared-out skirts) did
nothing to facilitate the esteem; and most of us are familiar with the
superior tone, somewhere between irritation and playfully mocking,
that in the right circles is elicited by this impostor-prophet, this gar-
ish and muddled showman, whose buzzwords are every
man-in-the-street's common coin—Gutenberg galaxy, "hot" and
"cold" media, message and massage, etc.—and whom no hard science type grants any seriousness or epistemological dignity. Truth to
tell, this pyrotechnician laid no claim to such recognition anyway: "I
explain nothing," he writes. "I explore. And logic is a term devoid
of meaning when applied to an explorer." It is a weakly coherent
theory internally, but the model for an "open" body of writings
recording in the tracings of their very syntax—mosaic-like, non-lin-
ear, hopping from subject to subject like a channel changer—the
novel electronic grammar it takes as its object. The cathode-ray
picture tube has its reasons Reason knoweth not, and McLuhan
manically defies reason to give a more truthful account of it.
Unverifiable sooth-sayings, undemonstrable rantings, excessive gen-
eralizations—all function, in his own terminology, "as the means of
probes." The phonetic alphabet as the source of Euclidian geometry,
papyrus "creating" the Roman Empire and Muslims "causing its
demise," "film [which] replaced the novel, the newspaper and the
theater all at once," and a hundred other pearls from the same bed,
would suggest a historian or sociologist of otherwise normal constitution in a state of near inebriation. This literature professor and
exegete of Joyce, Pound and Eliot was neither historian nor sociologist. Apart from their sense of subtlety, these high-flying
foreshortenings evoke a kind of technologically minded Malraux
who would apply to the world of material systems of representation
and inscription, and of signs, the same genius for the unlikely that
the author of *The Psychology of Art* applied to the world of forms.
All the same, beneath the oracular crust one finds that momentous
nugget which sums up in five words a hundred insights of venerable
authors: "the medium is the message." What we might call the
"mass mediology" of the sixties, smashed to bits by Bourdieu and
Passeron in a deservedly famous article, did not too precisely further
refine McLuhan's pronouncement.[8] The list of objections could be

---

[8] Pierre Bourdieu and Jean-Claude Passeron, "Sociologues des mythologies et
mythologies de sociologues," *Les Temps modernes*, 1962, p. 998.

and has been lengthened indefinitely: confusing technology itself with its usage makes of the media an abstract, undifferentiated force and produces its mirror image in an imaginary "public" for mass consumption; the magical naivete of supposed causalities turns the media into a catch-all and contagious "mana"; apocalyptic millenarianism invents the figure of a *homo mass-mediaticus* without ties to historical and social context, and so on. But as there can be sterile subtleties so can there be, as Descartes said, "fecund nonsense"—the McLuhanesque formulation being among that company. Mediology, which did not invent the equation and for good reason, seeks merely to drive it into its proper corner by giving it a content at once reasonable and radical. To conceive things at their extremes by expounding arguments pushed to the limit, following the Machiavellian recommendation, does not always preclude exact thinking.

Let us admit straightaway that the memorable phrase is not impervious to analysis. Umberto Eco, who does not however detest baroque art, was at no great pains to show in his *Cogito interruptus* of 1967 how McLuhan mixes together under the same label of *medium* the *channel* or material vehicle of information, the *code* or internal structure of a language, and the *message* or content of a concrete act of communication. Clearly our Canadian professor was unfamiliar with Saussure (and no less with Seignobos). Though it may also be that Thomas Aquinas' close reader Eco pays no heed to the complex materialities of the medium.[9] Whereupon arises this unfortunate symmetry: against the *medium minus code and message* of the McLuhanites, the semiologists set up *codes minus medium and milieu*. This was the way the founder of modern linguistics had wanted it, seeing no meaningful difference between a written and oral transmission (though *in his theory* subordinating written to oral): "Language and writing are two distinct systems of signs; the second exists for the sole purpose of representing the first."[10] "A pure social object that is indifferent to the matter or materiality of the signals

[9] Umberto Eco, *The Aesthetics of Thomas Aquinas*, tr. Hugh Bredin (Cambridge: Harvard University Press, 1988) (thesis in Aesthetics of 1954, originally published as *Il problema estetico in Tommaso d'Aquino*, 1956).
[10] Ferdinand de Saussure, *Course in General Linguistics*, tr. Wade Baskin (New York: McGraw-Hill, 1966), p. 23.

composing it" (Barthes, 1964), the code exists indifferently with respect to the material base of inscription and in constancy with respect to the channel of transmitting messages. With its methodological abstractness having become a metaphysical essentialism, semiology ended up correcting a technicizing abstraction with an intellectualist abstraction. To the *medium made into an absolute* (considered independently from the variety of messages it can carry, and from the intelligible order conferring meaning on them), answers back (settling its accounts) the *message made absolute*— a message without vehicle or vector, a semiological metamorphosis of divine being as *causa sui* existing in and for itself. The transporting of meanings takes place therefore without loss of energy; the textual machine runs without any motor or mobile parts. Within a given field of interpretive competencies, the message provides its own propulsion, self-regulated by its code. An all-star semiotics has thereby killed its two birds. It has shrugged off at once Nature (or the sign constituted as a real object in time and space) and politics (or the subject structured by surroundings). It is an edification in things got the wrong way round which reminds us that the dynamics of the message and the materiality of the base are either lost or found in tandem with one another. There have been some strange creatures christened in the Code's name. Given the status of objects are: language without material inscription, speech without phonation, text without book, film without camera or filmstrip, painting without canvas. In a word, the playing cards without the cards—summarized by only the *rules* of the game (poker, bridge, or belote). And in the category of subjects: the communicant without community, the message brought home without any mail handling costs or expenses for making its way there. We are presented with a manufactured knowledge whose basis and backdrop are missing the concrete networks of knowledge (labs, scientific community, procedures, congresses, journals, etc.), whose Reason lacks a sequence of inscriptions, and whose relationship of meaning has no relations of force. A supreme fiction of the work without tools or workers? This is the point at which semiology would truly have gone from one extreme to the other.

The "act of communication" that takes place between scriptor and reader, so precious to advocates of the "textual," puts a premium on a triple and perilous abstraction: 1) It abstracts from the long history of material operations and socio-technical systems, each of whose individual communicants is the end result (accounting for the point at which there is an "author," and isolated "reader," etc.). 2) It abstracts from the long history of cultural operations that determine and underlie acts assumed to be simple (the forms and modes of reading, looking, writing, gathering and retrieving, etc.). 3) It abstracts from the long history of political operations that have finally made possible the community of a code (through the fostering and management of a national language by means of a centralized power, promoting literacy, legislatively creating archives and other public stores, etc.).

The answer to the question "what is an author?" cannot afford to disdain the material form of the book (its size, binding, frontispiece, publisher's and printer's logo and colophon, etc.) and its legal fallout. So too with the "what is a text?" question: impossible to reckon as originary and natural the text's homogeneity, its stability, its conformity—later properties of the form writing took, and which appeared and became standard with industrial modernity. The idea of the author supposes that of the work as a unity of reference, and this latter unity assumes the further identifiable unity of the book as object. These are two assumptions that are unknown in the logosphere: the thirteenth-century *peciae* recited medleys, often without any author's name attached to them, and in the same collection they could alternate excerpts from diverse genres and authors, and sometimes in different languages. In France, we are told one must wait until the year 1400 to find, with the works of Guillaume de Machaut, a fully homogeneous text, one with clearly identified title and author.[11] In short, "author" and "text" are *results* and not *givens*. There is no "author" in the lay sense without a certain material culture of the book. And no autonomy of the "text" without all the variations of types and sizes of printed copies, without the development of a method for biblical commentary and inter-glossing by exegetes, without that long process of the separation of meaning from the first systems of material inscription of signs. It is in fact a process of abstraction whose apotheosis has unquestionably been marked by literary semiology.

A choice must be made to emphasize code or codex, the

---

[11] Paul Zumthor, *La Lettre et la voix* (Paris: Le Seuil, 1977), p. 123.

language system or its material embodiment, perhaps one will
say. But that's exactly what one had best avoid doing by carefully
examining watersheds and precise turning points. What good is
it to hock one fetishism for another—structure for material
implementation? The requisite formalizing of the code into a
"pure system of internal relations" led semiology to posit its
autonomy in order to better standardize its application. Now, for
one thing the existence of a code is not a condition necessary for
an act of communication, as we see plainly with the example of
painted or engraved pictures and all those non-verbal indices
that can accompany a verbal communication itself (sign language and facial expressions, gestures, intonation, etc. make
meanings): the code is thus not everything. And the sign's becoming *act* (its operativity) is, furthermore, conditioned by how it
becomes a *trace of memory*, or its material methods of inscription: the code does not therefore hold a monopoly on meaning.

8. The Force of Forms

Some have managed to present the semiotic turn as a *transition
from the what to the how*. We should not make of the mediological
turn simply a *return to the what* as the material condition of the
how. It would be to assume that the building obeys only the dictates
of the stone, and that "lapidary" style ordinarily hides raw materials. This overtilting of the balance would be a bit naive. It is true
that historians of the forms of writing scarcely separate any longer
systems of notation from a physics of their material base. The clay
"guides" cuneiform through the angle of the tracing tool used (it is
difficult to impress curves with a chisel, punch or stylus bevelled into
a burin). Papyrus documents, whose material base is vegetal, com-
pensate for this by making possible the sharpened reed stylus,
thereby favoring simplified and minimal systems of symbols and
characters, notably non-capitalization. Without our rehearsing the
transitions from stone to clay to papyrus to parchment to paper to
screen, each reader can imagine for himself how a Latin maxim
carved on the stone monument in a public place for collective reading in Rome will not call forth the same interpretation as the
identical sentence in the course of a letter of Cicero's. Likewise, the

meaning of a text is not to be found solely in its wording on the page. If "*form is meaning*" (in the bibliographer McKenzie's formulation), this means that the material is no matter of indifference. The simple choice of character, the size, the layout, the word-spacing, the paper quality, all have their own effective meanings, visual and tactile. And these forms of writing or printed pages preempt the social classification of what presents itself for reading (and thus how the reader will receive it). The contemporary researcher who calls up over great distances a "document" on-screen—dematerialized by its digitized transmission, disconnected from its first medium of manuscript and printed form, cut off from its original size and context—is extremely likely to decode it in an anachronistic way. We simply are not liable to apply the same exegesis to an article placed on page thirteen of the newspaper and the same article distributed over five columns on the front page; nor to a seventeenth-century text depending on its printing in a quarto or duodecimo edition. A poem will not resonate the same aesthetically when printed with or without its accompanying margins and blank spaces. The identical photograph printed on a quarter page of the tabloid and blown up into a four-by-three meter poster becomes two distinct pictures. Will the electronic libraries of the future invent a new breed of researcher, the immemorializing cyber-scholar, subtracted from the materialized memories of traditional archives?

These formal aspects of layout and design are *constitutive of the message itself*. There is in the rigor of semiological abstraction a propensity to shoulder the immemorial partition between the world of things and the world of spirit. In its estimation, the structures it brings to light come under the head of internal analysis; the surroundings and conditions of access it observes, of external analysis. It is the very validity of the check-point between physical exteriority and semantic interiority that has been thrown into doubt. Hasn't the time arrived to draw out all the epistemological consequences of discovering that the spirit of the age is as much in its objects as in its literary works, as much in our own hands as in our heads? There is a kind of spirit and intelligence in our vacuum cleaners, our automobiles, our telephones and our toothbrushes; and materiality in our symbolic goods. This *fin de siècle*'s *Zeitgeist* thrives as ubiquitously in the design of washbasins as in the displays of our bookstore shelves. It seems, say the designers, that our bathrooms changed their soul at the beginning of the seventies (ceasing to be the somber chamber in which one shuts oneself up to perform intimate ablutions). That is, at the cultural moment when the Freudian vulgate was entering the dailies, and certain analysts and analysands undertook to cast a curious eye on the basic functions covered by the national health organizations (why after all should that be shameful any longer?). Should we conclude that our furniture designers might also have been sitting in on Lacan's seminars?

As surroundings can have genius, so can the media of texts and representation take on spirit. That they have it more and more is evident in an industrial and post-industrial age. Here we would have to take up the carefully argued praise of textures, alloys and plastics to be found in the writings of a "materiologist" like François Dagognet. He has shown how in plastic creation "the idea germinates out of the basis of the material itself instead of imposing itself thereon" (the sculptor César is hardly one to deny that). Visual artists (who have practiced intuitively and for a long while McLuhan's adage) generally speaking are far ahead of the others on this score; we can have confidence in these silent Pythias of mediological messages. The celebration of raw materials by contemporary plastic artists, as by the industrial arts, are in their own way evidence that materials become in themselves intelligible forms in equal measure as the intellect takes on material form (or the reverse). In the past, the material bases for inscription of signs were inert, static like a sheet of paper. And already by the nineteenth century photosensitive film provided the know-how for conserving and storing a *visual* trace. An electromagnetic base medium accomplished the same for sound traces. Silicon and arsenicon of gallium added to these known properties powers of initiative and self-activation.[12] And the computer screen is a dynamic medium of inscription— interactive, user-friendly—that through the "electronic book" will transform our practices of reading, writing, and invention. A

---

[12] Preface to *La Matière de l'invention*, Centre Pompidou (Paris: Collection Inventaire, Paris 1979). See also, again by François Dagognet, *Pour l'art d'aujourd'hui. De l'objet de l'art à l'art de l'objet* (Paris: Dis voir, 1992).

silicon microchip can, all told, overturn "the order of discourse."*

What holds true for written text and philologists holds *a fortiori* for visual representation and its semiologists. The most intricate "syntagmatic" treatments of the narrative poetics of the film medium would err, I think, to spare themselves and us the trouble of studying beforehand the techniques for taking, projecting and distributing or broadcasting pictures. Ranging historically from frescoes to virtual reality graphics, visual representations do not indeed lend themselves to panoramic inclusion under a uniform discourse. Would that a brilliant visual semiotics not blot out too completely the more traditional craft-industrial study of the methods of manufacturing and numerous transformations of the magic lantern, or of the various recording media—tele-cinema (bringing films to the TV screen), kinescope (TV to movie screen), VCR, 16 mm synchronous sound, mobile car video, etc. For moving pictures in particular, one would do well not to proceed from the latter stage of significant forms but to *go back* from signification to the manufacture and production.

Once the technological moment of the process has been boiled off, vaporized literarily, one is doubtless left with a medium whose load has been lightened, a flexible and obliging medium. A "channel" transformed in this way into a simple vector for codes and distributor of messages is no longer a true *modus operandi*, and its users will feel free to make pass through it whatever they want (and not what the "channel" tolerates), without any particular damage or distortions. This sometimes has the effect of making the semiologist a spirited spokesman for modernity's delights. He is the herald of good news alone, especially for those of a more literary persuasion: "No need for

*See especially three recent essays that address the fate of the book in an era of cyberspace. Debray's paper "The Book as Symbolic Object" and André Bazin's "Towards Meta-Reading" were both presented at the San Marino conference on the Book in Spring 1994, sponsored by the Centro di Studi Semiotici e Cognitivi of the University of Bologna. They appear in a forthcoming anthology of essays based on presentations at that conference, entitled *The Future of the Book*, edited by Geoffrey Nunberg and published jointly by the University of California Press and Brepols. The third is Geoffrey Nunberg's well-balanced consideration of "The Places of Books in the Age of Electronic Reproduction," *Representations* 42 (Spring 1993), pp. 13–37. [Trs.]

concern, things will turn out alright."[13] Those who profess an interest in our practices of mediation can expect from this the ideal conformist discourse (everyone in the same boat, nothing new under the semiological sun). The medium conceived (or forgotten) as an auxiliary organ confirms the glorious and received idea (around since the dawn of philosophy) that man is his own center, the master of nature as of his tools. Ancestral hierarchies turn out to be validated in subtle ways, in values just as they are in academic course programs. The secular distinction still holds between the liberal arts, having speech for their object, and the mechanical arts, which are concerned with the material world. It is duplicated by that between the *normative* disciplines, which establish order in the secret grammar of signs, and the *descriptive* disciplines, which focus on physical or morphological phenomena—paleography, epigraphy, source studies of texts, etc. Has not the low-profile and parallel (or subsidiary) role played recently by the School of Paleography and Archival Studies (the Ecole des chartes) at the Sorbonne predisposed us to accept this separation between (humble) research in the diachronic materialities of the documented word and (noble) research in the synchrony of Codes? Though the semiologist insists that a language does not have an author, he grudgingly perpetuates the "satellitization" of meaning around a queenly consciousness. Language may de-center meaning, but speech re-centers it on the subject of the act of utterance, a conscious and undetermined subject. Faced with this, the mediologist will not even be able to resort to those newfound potentialities that result from every Copernican-style revolution, since he neither displaces nor reverses the center of gravity of the universe of symbols (from a point closer to home to another more distant). He is content to point out that there is a plurality of different machines (and not *The* Machine), and that they restrict us in identifiable ways (without being sovereign or supernatural). Says the semiologist: "Confronted with the anonymous divinity of technological Communication, our answer might be, 'May *our* will be done, not thine'" (Umberto Eco). Wavering somewhere between

---

[13] Umberto Eco, "N'ayez pas peur de la télévision," *Le Nouvel Observateur*, 2 Sepember 1983.

extremes, the mediologist vis-à-vis the medium sends forth a more pedestrian prayer: "Let us look for the least objectionable conciliation possible between thy requisites and our requests." Codes can be playfully juggled with, but not machines. And pridefulness having first been lost when the Order of Language was instituted, the enthusiasts of the signifier rediscover it in the end in their jubilant linguistic point-scoring and game-playing. They might say we are no longer like gods because we do not invent the rules of the game—but demigods, yes, nonetheless, for these rules *are* transparent to us and we get the better of them. Constrained to greater modesty, the mediologist will even hesitate to sign up to the idea so skillfully developed by Michel de Certeau, that "custom carries communication." He will find it hard to celebrate with quite the same verve as this author of the *Arts de faire* the creativity of independent local radio stations, the lived spontaneity of instances of *bricolage*, and the various ways in which local resistances maintain themselves by means of officials on the take. He will no doubt follow Certeau in drawing a distinction between a "popular culture" with its impregnable rainbow patchworks, and a homogenizing "mass culture." But he will resist seeing in the first of these cultures an assured road to salvation, or a subversion of the One by the Many. Without exactly lowering his head in deference to the technological megasystem, he is sure that the believing, knowing and acting subject finds there a powerful opponent, and that hard tech can be mollified but not domesticated. For it is not enough to exert a legalistic control over the network in order to control the tenor of the messages. An amusing translation of this claim: if we could imagine a France in which the Revolutionary Communist League, on the day following a Great Victory, were to take over the national TV network T.F.1, the program director Mr Alain Krivine would very quickly come to resemble the father and son team of the Bouygues.

The bearer of news this dismal runs little risk of overdosing on accolades and hurrahs—no matter how demoralizing some of our optimisms or bracing our pessimisms.

III

Philosophical Terrain

Perhaps I will be recognized as competent to direct research *in philosophy*. Were this to be the case, I could not help being especially receptive to such recognition, given that the laborers of mediological groundwork toil in an ill-reputed, indeed unsavory, non-place. They are the proletarians of the City of Philosophy. I came to understand only belatedly why viewing religious history mediologically held no interest for historians of religion; why those in art history circles feel it to be no concern of theirs when the naive self-evidences of their historically brief notion of "art" are re-thought in a new perspective; nor the specialists of political science when a mediology of the State, parties, or doctrines proposes a similar reconceptualization. As to philosophy, I cannot help thinking that what is invisible to professional reviews, and the "no comment" of the titled commentators, translates (despite some magisterial exceptions) a collegial and even hereditary blindness. Mediology elevates to the level of a genuine theoretical issue what a philosophical tradition of the innate ideas type holds to be a banal matter of subsidiary intendancy. The pragmatics of thought being what we prefer least to think about, our bad objects are, rather, conceptual non-objects. Whoever looks for the "through," the "between," the "by," the "with"—all of these mere means with which we make do, lowly residues of the Logos—is rummaging through the trash bins of Thought. No favored son of heaven, we find him betrothed to disdaining the Verb for the adverbs, nouns for clauses, or the beginning for the

subsequent incarnations.[1] We are warranted in supposing that
this much indifference betrays a kind of denial (perhaps, one day,
it would be worth psychoanalyzing a few systems of reasoning to
bring to light the "mediological repressions" belonging to each).

1. "Ways In Which We Still Revere"

It is the metaphysics of Light, it seems to us, that contributed the
most to render classical Reason blind to its own instruments. It
has helped make practical mediations that are outside logic into
the remaindered goods left out of the inventories of our grand
philosophies of Being and the Subject. The bright glare of "the
torch of Truth": was this not the other name for that most venerable torch of the world, the Godhead-Sun? Reason is Light,
and all light comes from Jupiter or our Eternal Father. For a
Dionysus the Areopagite, positivistically speaking, God was an
incandescent source of light and warmth, and the entire Creation
a luminous expansion outward from this central sun. A hoary
theme, this radiating continuity between Being and beings that
allows sinners to participate in the divine glory. Here and there
the radiating primal Logos admits "relays"—angels, apostles or
an angelic Doctor—but the immaterial emanation traverses all of
these transmitters in a straight line, as if they were transparent
glass, without the need to correlate discrepant measurements
that take account of parallax. In just this way too the Holy
Spirit speaks through the prophets, and Truth through the
mouths of children, losing nothing in the translation. Nothing
goes astray nor gets erased in the Divinity's e-mails. One can,
like the Calvinists, emphasize the incommensurability between a
sovereign God and His creatures without altering the shared
nature between God and men. For the latter are joined together

---

[1] "Traditional philosophy speaks through nouns or verbs, not through relations;
thus it always begins with a divine sun that illuminates everything, with a beginning
that is going to be deployed in a history that is finally given a name . . . " (Michel
Serres, *Éclaircissements* [Paris: François Bouvin, 1992], p. 150.) [A translation has
recently been published as "Conversations on a Life in Philosophy," in Michel Serres,
with Bruno Latour, *Conversations on Science, Culture, and Time*, tr. Roxanne
Lapidus (Ann Arbor: University of Michigan Press, 1995). Trs.]

from within by the same source of brightness which spreads the fountainhead and countenance of beneficent Light as far as to the tiniest glimmer of Augustinian consciousness. As Progress became the Providence of those who no longer believed in Providence, Reason (capitalized) will have perhaps proven the compensatory goddess for those no longer believing in God-Light. There is dormant science in religions and mythologies—by which we can account for the thoroughly practical interest of theologies. But are there not as well many myths in our sciences? No one claims that in every philosopher there is a theosopher waiting to burst out, because Reason as a substantial entity is a degraded myth, a more popular consequence of the work of learning in its guise as a going beyond the sensory, and of reason as an infinite task seeking to return to the unconditioned. Everyone can acknowledge, however, that the bridges were *not* completely burned, at the beginning of the modern age, between scientific research and mystical traditions—to say nothing of Newton and his passions for alchemy—no more than between Illuminism and our Enlightenment.

As far back as its Greek roots, the optical metaphor pegs idea [*eidos*] to visible form and knowledge to vision—of all five senses the one predestined to the theoretical because removed (unlike taste, touch, and smell) from all materiality. Even if the classical theory of seeing makes it into a kind of palpation at a distance of the object by the eye, and all perception into the meeting of two beams of light from opposite directions, the form of the straight line remains the norm. But each ray is exposed to being deviated or refracted by the milieu or medium it crosses, a deviation that will supply the "false idea." Out of this comes the interest in emptying out the space between the understanding and its object. To elucidate is to hollow out [to "en-void," *évider* in French] everything found in the middle or milieu to obtain the evidence, a rectitude willfully recovered more or less laboriously. To intuit means to see the intelligible "live." No doubt to behold "purely" is a reward, the crowning gesture of an active asceticism—an ascending dialectic, conversion of the spirit, methodical doubt. Yet the ideal at once rector, connector and director remains the ray of light, Reason's official emblem (especially educational Reason). Whatever the initial

difficulties of idealist clarification, the final metaphors of illumination, unveiling, not to say bedazzlement, bespeak the exact
opposite of co-produced meanings.

Along the usual scale of values that descend from brightness to
gloom (among the latter, Nietzsche's "somber man" and Freud's
"dark mud"), salvation resides in the soul's re-ascent toward the
light (because the fire of human looking upon the sacred is extin-
guished in those who dwell in darkness), above and beyond the
effects of optics and filters. Being's immediate revelation to
thought will be all the easier in proportion as it is disencumbered
of intermediaries. A direct access to the luminous Source that
gnosticism and the pagan doctrines of salvation reserved to a
handful of initiates: this is what Christianity offered to all
through its exoteric deployment of the Scriptures, the means by
which Christos' sect achieved a revolution. It was a sect that can
be considered to have democratized the esoteric by bringing
about a universal access to the origin of all light, opening a gate
that had until that time been bolted shut, an act that the
Enlightenment can be held to have taken a step further by smash-
ing the fetters of truth as Revelation. This was a profanation of
the contents of the old truth, but not really of its temple or of the
basic outlines for acceding to the sanctuary (which was spontaneously conceived as a triumphant lifting of the veils). Voltaire's
allegorical Reason dispels prejudices much as the light of day dis-
sipates the darkness. The metaphor of dawn—exciting even
though or precisely because ever postponed to the morrow—
gives this "divine" rationalism its beautiful and tenacious
ingenuity: what obscurantism will ever hold out against the rise
of a new day? Or what ayatollah against a geometry book? Or
war against a school? The true's transcendence of the process
leading to its discovery and of disputes concerning its appropriation, internalizes the truth, a self-immanent light. Free of the job
of concrete application, unexposed to external system malfunc-
tions and glitches, holding forth all at once the code, the public,
and the channel to any person who knows how to reason—these
are all characteristics equally attributed to perpetual motion, to
making one's way across a nonexistent space, to transportation
without a vehicle. Sun, God, Reason: the three metaphors of
Truth's self-institution form a sort of cinematic cross fading

sequence (across theological, metaphysical, and positive eras, speaking in Comtian terms).

Everything the light metaphor saves us from having to conceptualize is not hard to see. Light has miraculous virtues: it is dispensed freely, clean, immaterial, simple, straight, direct and nearly instantaneous, without becoming degraded or deviated, with no parasites or static, without delay and recurrence. A material system of transmission necessarily degrades information. But there is no "noise" in light, and illumination excludes alteration. Ideal (non-)transmission has a zero-sum effect on the contents. Light basically enables one to evade the implications of entropy. Everything has to be bought and paid for here below, except a ray of sunlight. There is an equal quantity of photons at the emission end and at the reception end. Whereas, if I "emit" in Paris today, let us say, three hundred printed pages, and I return one year later to the zone of distribution, it is highly probable that they will have disappeared into a quasi black-hole (a library catalogue), or that they will have lost—after their circulation, relaying and assimilation have been brought about by such and such a "pocket" in the videosphere—nine tenths of their semantic charge. Any author of a recently published work can experience this dissipation in the course of a single month: when the book is taken up by reviewers it can look like betrayal (its novelty is cut down to size by tradition, it is lumped together with inappropriate notions and wrong contexts, reduced to cliche, exorbitantly simplified, etc.) In every imaginable way, the initial energy is dispersed into the gradations of the mediaspheric particle-stream, in totality or partially.

Light's ideal radiancy, furthermore, is the same everywhere: dispersed uniformly along the earth's entire surface, cast on poor and rich alike, Zulus and Anglophones, with equal reflectiveness (in the mental mirrors of humankind). A homogeneity that neutralizes places and spaces to the advantage of a field of distribution without real qualities, an ether devoid of accidents and, on this score, rather roguishly universal. The logocentrism that so readily abstracts from mental landscapes and techno-cultural contexts gets on marvelously with the light-metaphysics model of symbolic propagation.

Some scholar will perhaps one day follow the trail of the motif of sunbeams in our metaphysical tradition, from Plato's Cave to Freinet of the Freinet School.[2] It is between Fénelon and Voltaire's day, toward the end of classicism, that we see a toppling of the semantic regime of this metaphor derived from mysticism. Over this time, Grace made a fall into intelligence, but did so as if the modernity of the plural elucidations of the Enlightenment altered the affective valence of Light itself. It is as though, through a kind of new equilibrium, no sooner were the solar symbols to represent the French monarch as God's delegate abandoned in favor of his actual portrait, at the end of the seventeenth century, than a kind of compensatory representation of Reason in the form of the sun became common practice. It was shown beaming everywhere its invincible rays, fanning out in all directions, in a radiant typographical display formed by characters and figures, numbers and the etched lines of illustrations from engraved plates. This change of register from sacred to profane has apparently no ill effects on the innate stability of wave lengths between the sender of truths and their recipient—the justification in principle permitting the model of *natural* solar radiation. If God exists and Adam is his creature, Father and son spontaneously tune in to one another. No need for interpreters or dictionaries in Eden when Adam and Eve speak the same language as their creator. Original sin and the fall of the Tower of Babel will not impede natural light from re-directing faculties more or less beclouded by prejudices and bodily needs toward those paths leading back to a lost yet indelible affinity. This is the source of the serene optimism of a rationalism that, however much it had to give up the idea of a personal God or a transcendent principle as with Spinoza, has always found it hard to accord positivity to the false (Spinoza: "error consists in the deprivation of knowledge alone"), and so easy to assume the efficacy of the good and true ("*omne bonum est diffusivum sui*"). The true idea includes its own distinction and propagation ("*Verum index sui et falsi*"). With or without a divine guarantee, this sovereign power of the human mind, shorn of all alloys and

---

[2] Nanine Charbonnel has been busy sifting through this vast corpus in her highly revealing scrutiny of the founding figural "as ifs" of the European identity (Centre de recherche sur les métaphores et les modèles). See her *La Tache aveugle*, in three volumes: *Les Aventures de la métaphore*, *L'Important, c'est d'être propre*, and *Philosophie du modèle* (Strasbourg: Presses Universitaires de Strasbourg, 1993).

prostheses, has, if you will, the faculty of materializing without materials—an ontological aptitude erstwhile reserved to God and now politely ceded retroactively to the idea in its adequateness. One doesn't fit a sunbeam with prosthetic devices; if anything, one clears away the surrounding underbrush to mark out a neat place for it. So that the Platonic Cave's pupils might turn their attention and heads in the good direction, the Teacher will see to it that everything be removed which obfuscates, that heavy curtain of superstitions and the vain seduction of machines. (In such a way did abbot Suger wish to contract the space of load-bearing walls in Saint Denis in order to unshackle the light's entry into the nave, synonymous with that of God into the hearts of the faithful.)

Had the humanist label been invoked too unthinkingly whenever "the technology that dehumanizes the world" was deplored? Would not technology rather have de-divinized, disenchanted, obscured and soiled that world by positioning itself between Nature and ourselves, or between ourselves and our own previous existence (in the Platonic dialogue of the soul with itself)? Everything that is thus "intercalated," all the way from the invention of writing to the machine, slows up or impedes the *adaequatio rei et intellectus*. Including Rhetoric, Eloquence, and Poetics, those superfluities or merely literary deceptions. To plane down signs to a uniform surface, consign the role of relays to the sidelines, minimize the channels of *transmitting* meanings—these would be the tacit battle cries of the True and its idealism.

A cavalier synopsis, of course, put so summarily. I have referred to exceptions, and in truth they are considerable. Do we not find in Plato a mediologist, even though (or perhaps *because*) he had taken such a dislike to the new medium of his time? The myth of Toth in *Phaedrus* dramatizes the most famous and ambiguous of mediological analyses of writing—that accursed alphabet which Aeschylus' Zeus chastizes Prometheus for having given to Man along with fire—in terms of a dangerous (or more exactly, ambivalent or "pharmaceutical") mediation. The theorized subordination of the mechanical to the logical (in geometry) and the scorn for material technique perhaps tilted attention in the Greek world toward *the techniques of intellect*. The care Aristotle took in founding side-by-side with his *Organon* an autonomous Rhetoric, equidistant from Logic and sophistic, reveals an effort to account for the technics of persuasive discourse in a properly philosophical vocabulary. But one would surely have to visit the works of Hegel, and the full range of epics of mediation we owe them: aesthetical, logical, historical, philosophical. The placing of the mind outside itself constitutes man's being as becoming, a drama of Spirit's "other-becoming" that includes mediation as a rupture in the definition of the universal.[3] Consciousness' displacement into the written trace sees attributed to it a genetic power—of objective history, of the State, of the Law. Yet it is Hegelian Spirit's obligation and destiny to overcome all mediations so as to be capable of returning unto itself and feeling everywhere in its own element. One mounts higher along the value scale of mediations, too, in proportion to their immateriality. Just as the *Aesthetics* has us pass from the external and massive spatiality of the Egyptian pyramid to the internal temporality of Romantic poetry, sandwiched by the internalized space of classical painting, the *Encyclopedia* elevates us, in the odyssey of signs or "representations of the intelligence," from the still heavy spatial figure of the hieroglyph to alphabetic writing, with its signs of signs, and thence to "sonorous language," to the temporal unfolding of the voice as a spiritual element of thought.[4] Hearing becomes therefore to sight what poetry is to painting: a lever of the sublime through its wrenching of the mind free of materiality. It is well known, finally, how in his *Origin of Geometry* Edmund Husserl re-legitimized the technical system of inscription as a condition making possible scientific ideality; and how from that starting point Jacques Derrida has patiently rid metaphysical postulates of presence and voice to thematize the insurmountable mediation of the trace. Alphabetical notation ceases from then on to be the Logos' all-purpose handmaiden, the appearance of essence, the outside of an inside: that is, the simple graphic derivation of an origin, the dead supplement of a living speech.

[3] Bernard Bourgeois, *La Pensée politique de Hegel* (Paris: Presses Universitaires de France, 1969).

[4] G.W.F. Hegel, *Philosophy of Mind, Translated from "The Encyclopedia of the Philosophical Sciences"*, tr. William Wallace (Oxford: Oxford University Press, 1894), §458 (in Sub-Section C, "Psychology"), p. 458. See Jacques Derrida, "The Well and the Pyramid, Introduction to Hegel's Semiology," *Margins of Philosophy*, tr. Alan Bass (Chicago: Chicago University Press, 1982).

2. Emerging at the Wrong Place:
Historical Materialism

It is only with the advent of materialism in the last century, however, that we would have just cause to anticipate the sharpest break with the solar immediacy of the true. Had not the young Marx hoped it would come? 1845, *The German Ideology*: "Philosophers did nothing more than interpret the world in countless ways: what matters is to transform it." This exhortation failed, alas, to confront its own conditions of possibility. What must philosophy become if it would transform something other than the history of philosophy? Which mediations does this leap ahead insist upon? We are left with a finality without strategy, a program minus a concept. The great Marx did not give himself the means to his end. This was because the young Marx, in respect to symbolic efficacy, was born old. As if in his pastoral he dated from a time before Balzac and even before Diderot, like a Man of Light rather than of the Enlightenment. He seems to conceive of theory's efficacy through an inverted (and thus preserved) Spinozist grid: the order of ideas being adequate formally to the order of things. In the case of Spinoza, the pure idea being the very idea itself of being, it cannot but return to the precinct it comes from. With Marx, the true theory of class war is supposed to come back to the class producing history's driving force "with the same necessity as the laws that preside over the metamorphoses of nature." The historical process is self-reflexive: its passive synthesis is theoretical, its active synthesis practical. This mirroring structure makes for a virtuous circle summed up laconically by the classical declaration, "Without revolutionary theory, no revolutionary movement; without revolutionary movement, no revolutionary theory." As Lenin will say, "Marxism is all-powerful because it is true." It would not be the science of history if it did not realize itself in history, and it would not realize itself in history if it were not the science of it. Idealist predestination thus nourished during almost a century an infinity of materialist tautologies of the type: "Marxist-Leninist philosophy *represents* the proletarian class struggle in theory, and the theory and the proletarian class struggle *represent* philosophy within theory." Or even more, this: "According to principle, true ideas always serve the people; false ideas always serve the people's enemies"—which are words not from Saint Thomas nor Saint Theresa, but from Althusser. This philosopher, my teacher and friend, who held "the fusion of Marxist theory and the workers' movement to be the greatest event of all of human history," paid little attention to the accidental conditions of this mystical fusion, namely the panoply of means and vectors of *representation* that were supposed by the *a priori* surprising co-penetration of esoteric theorems and lines of striking workers. There is not, to my knowledge, any serious Marxist history of the history of Marxism, and this is not by chance: as I tried to show with my chapter titled "Marxist Idealism" in *Le Scribe*, and especially in "Self-Propelling Practice," Marxism had taken itself out of the running as far as thinking through its own incarnation in terms other than a string of eventful moments [*péripétie*], the return of self to self in which the cultural, political, and technical mediations (developed by the workers' movement) figure the journey necessary for essence to be reconciled with phenomena, the mere delay required by necessity in order to make itself actuality. Marx had dreamed of a world without intellectuals or apparatchiks, without imagery or idolatry, where his ideas would have been able to become "material force" by taking hold of the masses, according to his formulation, without lowering themselves into "marx*ism*" (a term at the outset pejorative for the first Marxians of the International). No place could be found for happenstance or material contingency—which *do*, in a sense, comprise the invention of an engineer, the rotary press, the railroad or the electric telegraph. The theory that declared its familiarity with the meaning and direction of History cared little for the means by which to make itself known, in the here and now. The Marxian opus did however have to clear a way for itself, to lay paths of incursion—through a dense undergrowth of highly competitive messages—to thrive and survive in the midst of wild beasts, to invent for itself its own networks of conversion, cobble together its supporting props of propulsion (inventories of images, emblems, foundation myths, hagiographies, ceremonials, etc.). Otherwise put: to manufacture a tradition, in the form of a *singular milieu of transmission* built up around a certain number of procedures for recognition and mutual familiarity or working knowledge (congresses, summarized reports and concise hand-books, cells, reviews, newspapers, research centers, colloquia, etc.). Becoming a Marxist meant joining this orchestra, for which the musical score paradoxically reserved no place. Nor did it allot independent existence to a priestly class, a pantheon of heroes, sanctuaries and pilgrimages, mausoleums and rituals. All these are measures of vulgarization if you will, relegated by the founding minds to the bottom of the page, like some marginal theme for specialists of the lowly level beneath the street, for historians, chroniclers, or administrators, but without any possible retroactive effect on theory farther back upstream in time. Did not the terms "vulgate" and "vulgar Marxism" have a pejorative value for Marxologists? Christianity thematized the mystical body, charismatic transmission of authority, catechism and pastoralia, liturgy and apologetics—that is, its vectors of incarnation as much imaginary as institutional, just as it enthroned and made official the Vulgate through organizing a Council. As to the authorities of Marxism—a religion as inconsistent as it is involuntary—they did not reflect how it was to take bodily and collective form, and the constraints that follow from that. In the absence of such reflection, an ambitious doctrine saw itself out-flanked *a posteriori* by a pragmatism for current consumption dubbed "agitprop." The book by Serge Tchakhotin entitled *The Violation of Crowds by Political Propaganda*, published in 1939, gives a naive but symptomatic insight on its workings. Too bad Marx did not study in greater depth the history of religions. He would have learned in particular that ecclesiology is decisive in matters of theology. He might even perhaps have admitted, if not wished, the practice of his posthumous deification, though a little precipitate. The Indian king Asoka began to institute Buddhism three centuries after the Buddha. The latter was a sage who had professed atheism; the grand Vehicle of doctrine made him a God in the aftermath. Gods have their custom of triumphing over sages in the mind of peoples, to the point of deifying the agnostic wise men whom they are intent on making popular.

Nothing less materialist, on balance, than this philosophical materialism. Doubtlessly there are indeed behind ideas objective forces and stakes. And certainly the ideological controversies are presented as material relations of force. But this materiality belongs to the social relations in which the debates over ideas are entangled, and not to the mode of transmission and incorporation of the ideas themselves. These exist in peoples' heads, not physically. Marx respects the great divisions between subject and object, reproduction and production. The material is held to be present where serious things take place: in production and infrastructure. Wherever there are discourses, forms, and ideas, in superstructures, machines and materials fade out. Or at least in the conception of the whole, since in the margins of his doctrine this formidable journalist was an accomplished mediologist—for example when it came to Greek art and mythology:

> Is the intuition of nature and of social relations that is at the base of the Greek inspiration compatible with spinning looms, locomotives and the electric telegraph? What does Vulcan represent compared with Robert and Co., Jupiter next to the lightening rod, and Hermes beside *Crédit Mobilier*? What becomes of Fama faced with Printinghouse Square [where the offices of the *Times* were located]?[5]

Or further:

> Up to now it has been thought that the Christian myth-building during the Roman Empire was possible only because printing had not yet been invented. The truth is altogether different. The daily press and the telegraph, which spread their inventions over the whole earth in a second, fabricate more myths (and the bourgeois cattle believe and spread them) in one day than could formerly have been done in a century.[6]

[5] Introduction to *L'Esquisse d'une critique de l'économie politique* (1857), in Marx and Engels, *Études philosophiques* (Paris: Editions sociales, 1974). The remark's context is classically evolutionist. [Debray quotes Marx's comment from an introduction to Marx's text in French that does not appear in the English translation, K. Marx, *A Contribution to the Critique of Political Economy*, tr. S. W. Ryazanskaya and ed. Maurice Dobb (London: Lawrence & Wishart, 1970 and New York: International Publishers, 1970). Trs.]

[6] Karl Marx, Letter to Ludwig Kugelman (in Hanover), London, July 27, 1871, in Saul K. Padover, tr. and ed., *The Letters of Karl Marx* (Englewood Cliffs: Prentice-Hall, 1979), p. 282.

But inside the theory, like the Aristotelian who Benveniste tells us confused certain categories of language for categories of thought, the Marxist was unaware that he sublimated the blast furnace into a Proletariat; sublimated into a "vanguard element of the working class" the reader of a daily or the subscriber to the monthly review *Les Cahiers du communisme*; into the "coming to consciousness about exploitation" a certain competence for deciphering a bookish common knowledge; and into the "union of theory and practice" certain channels of contact within an organization that rested on the dominance of print culture and of an inscription system based in paper (including the popular university, the commonly consulted handbook, the communist cell library, the discussion in party congresses of theses and printed platforms, the Marxist Week of the Book, the newspaper advancing the interests of a certain class as "collective organizer," etc.). At a distance from where we now stand, do not those redemptive figures of the advanced worker and party intellectual take on the appearance of imprints fleetingly set down by the march of technologies in the mud of class societies?

I attempted in *Cours de médiologie générale* to describe the ecological niche of socialism in its diverse branchings. The concept of graphosphere gives an intelligible unity to this century of lead (I am speaking of typeface characters, typesetting and Linotype). Absolutely no one leaps over the horizon of their own times. Marx put his black marks on paper at the pivotal point of a transition between the mechanical age (prolongation of the human muscular system) and the age of energetics (extension of the system of natural forces). We who are astride a second juncture—between machines designed to produce movement and those designed to produce information (extension of the nervous system)—cannot reproach Marx and company for having taken little notice of the mediological bedrock of the project of emancipation (as we doubtless are unaware of our own). One can simply express regret that this materialist idealism does not seem to have given urgency to the idea of making the chronologies tell us something new, by, for instance, placing in relation the birth of the First International (1864) and the invention of rotary presses (1860). Or beyond that, by relating, in France, the Teaching League (1866), the surge in circulation of the *Petit Journal*, furthered by the rotary press of Marinoni (from 50,000 copies in 1859 to 600,000 in 1869), and the laying of the transatlantic cable (1866). A literal-literate technology stipulates, in order to reach the collective memory, a carefully controlled level of skills (reading/writing, decoding/encoding), a collection of selective competencies. In addition, if one wanted to found a party in those days, one founded a newspaper to serve as the home base and central meeting place of the projected political avant-garde. This molding and role-modeling formation—that is to say, the collective of writers that the old-style newspaper represented, with the situation of the articles "being put to bed" as the linking "hyphen" and meeting ground between executives, printers and intellectuals—appeared wholly natural and eternal at the time, naturally eternal.* In a later period, however, as Bernard Stiegler has shown, analogically recorded memories drastically modify the "hand" dealt to us. Photography, phonography, film, radio, TV (to say nothing of digitized recording techiques) no longer require any particular qualification to be admitted to the archives, delegate the tasks of encoding and decoding to machines, give a comparative advantage to information over knowledge (to the document over criticism, to the event over duration, etc.). They "decommunitarize" knowledge and science even as they atomize and delocalize the collectives of knowledge (including the "collective intellectuals" that workers' parties were supposed to be).[7]

In principle, whoever reads a letter can also write them, and whoever receives them can also send them. But the person who looks at his radio receiver has no transmitter at his disposal; the person who tunes in or turns on a television broadcast cannot produce another one in return. Separating as it does devices for recording the original events from devices with which their traces

---

*The term in French for which I have substituted "being put to bed" is "*le marbre*" (the "marble"). This misnomer-metonymy, derived from print technology, refers to the polished cast iron tray, mounted on a frame, on which impositions and editing of texts took place. A book or article "on the marble" meant it was ready to be printed. In newspaper parlance, "avoir du [to have some] marbre" alluded to articles whose type characters had been composed but that because of space limitations had to lie in place awaiting subsequent printing. [Trs.]

[7] Bernard Stiegler, "Le droit, la technique, l'illetrisme," *Actions et recherches sociales*, June 1988, no. 2. See also "Mémoires gauches," *La Revue philosophique*, June 1990.

are received, the "industrialization of memory" (Stiegler's phrase) could not do otherwise than affect how individuals might be implicated civically and militantly who have become more and more passive and atomized. The library's crossover/expansion into a media center (done to upgrade its image) marks a change of "element" Marxist culture has been no more able to survive than the "industrial proletariat" has survived the shift from steel to polymers, or internal combustion engine to microprocessor. The faith based in Light metaphysics which hides from historical actors their own technological surroundings conceals from them as well the consequences of those surroundings' disappearance from consciousness.

It comes down to the fact that this giant of human thought who thought about neither mediation (the Party), nor mediators (party cadres) nor milieus (like that of the intelligentsia), nor the means (of distribution), was the least political of theoreticians. The author of *Capital* would not have been able, I think, to adequately explain to himself the power that this mobilizing *-ism* would one day exert over hundreds of millions of men, nor the formidable dynamism that it was to instill at its peak in underdeveloped and pre-capitalist countries. The hybrid of idea and motor [*l'idéo-moteur*] becomes an enigma from the moment ideology is made into a shadow game. Does not a slogan such as "religion is the opiate of the people" reveal two regrettable instances of ignorance—of opiate addicts first, of soldier-monks beyond that? Had Marx traveled a bit further, he would have known that the person who gives himself or herself to opium lays down the weapons or tools and stretches out, and tone and energy levels drop. The person given over, by contrast, body and soul to God intends all too well to make others profit from Him too. There ensues a characteristic and even characterological hyperactivity. As a general rule, religious faith is a tonic; the opium poppy a sedative. The Knights Templar of long ago, and today the hezbollahs or Muslim brethren, do not bear a very close resemblance to emaciated hookah-addicts in Chinese drug dens. Surely we can make this opposition to idealist belief in the omnipotence of ideas, itself still idealistic, undergo a profit-and-loss review that will show some pluses. Marxism remains a safeguard, particularly for us producers of signs who are always tempted to imitate the roosters in the fable that, atop their little mounds of fertilizer, think each morning their crowing makes the sun rise. The counter-song that would drown out the Marxists is well-known by now: the drowning of priests during the French Revolution can be laid at the Rousseau's doorstep, the seeds of the Gulag are to be found in *Capital* as is May '68 in Marcuse, and long live Solzhenitsyn—the Saint Michael of the Communist dragon. To help resist the too simple idea that ideas steer the world, it is not always a bad thing to hear oneself be reminded that ideology can be defined as "the dominant material relations going under the form of ideas." The Protestant heresy in the sixteenth century, put in this framework, was not the *source* of anything: it translated into representations the upsurge and advance of the bourgeoisie. Ideological illusion, the doctrine then adds, means taking the effect for the cause, affirming the existence of some intrinsic force of thought, when this force is actually loaned to it from outside by the massive energies of history. The movement of ideas thus does not contain its principle in itself, except in the eyes of the ideologues it blinds. To which the mediologist can respond further, yes, thought as such is not a practical operator, but thought as such does not exist either. Every social body of thought is a device for battle, and takes effect through its particular milieu. Marxism took at face value the idealist definition of thought as subjective determination, having its only seat in the brain of individuals, without grasping that an ideological corpus is not separable from the institutional corporate organization that shelters it, that it has produced and that it produces. Briefly and put in its own language: without grasping that a process of thought possesses the *objective materiality of an organizational process*. The Protestant heresy did not first take place in the minds of the faithful, only subsequently in a second phase to engender pastors, temples, synods, Geneva, and burnings at the stake. It was right away besieged by and within collective practices of organization: the two moments make only one.

The official attendant or deliverer of new emergences is called "prophet"; a "learned scholar" or scientist [*savant*] is the name for the official responsible for writing things up and critical reviews [*comptes rendus*]. The first propels his word forward to what lies ahead, proffers what he believes *should* be, restricts himself to a subject-to-subject relation. The second does not have to take in his charge the future of men; he says what being is in the present, describes relations between objects. In Karl Marx, the journalist was more penetrating than the economist, but the prophet took himself for a scholar-sage (which he was also), who in this instance was turned rather toward the natural than social sciences (in this the rival of Darwin). Science is oblivious to *-isms* and never refers itself to a founding father. It was logical that Marx should proclaim loud and clear he was not a Marxist. The result: practical mediology has conducted its business when the back of his child, Marxism, was turned, and played rather a dirty trick. One can detect in this posthumous return of the repressed the bitter revenge of what, for socialism, were mere communication or propaganda channels going under the name of "drive belts" [*courroies de transmission*].

If I bring up here this too well-known story, it is not only that it was my generation's story and by extension my own. A Marxist indeed I was, although no marxologist, right up to around 1968, when "the question of the nation" to which this tradition of thought brings only the most perfunctory answers, hit me, as well as my comrades, tragically, with blinding obviousness. Let us leave aside this story, which was a more edifying aid toward writing the *Critique of Political Reason* than for the texts here submitted for accreditation. I nonetheless mention the dominant inspiration of that historical moment because it was by looking back, in the seventies, not at the true thought of Marx but, rather simplemindedly, flatly and empirically, at the type of relations which had proven able to be forged between States or parties and a theory that had never been the concern of parties and States, that I was, lo and behold, constrained to conceptual exile. Discovering the improbable void of a theory of history without history— "Marxism nowhere to be found," as Daniel Lindenberg was calling it— obliged me to turn this to advantage by looking elsewhere. I could no longer play the devoted cleric-intellectual struggling his whole life to make the Hugolian Mouth of Darkness speak from within the infinite commentary of a corpus of texts at once obscure and forever fastened shut in its completed circle. "Everything has been said but nothing is clear?" No, it was in fact quite clear, yet concerning mediations by institutions and technologies *nothing was said*. It was the marginal mavericks of Marxism, its second cousins or dissidents, publicists and activists who had been rubbed the wrong way in the course of their humble tasks propagandizing for the organization who, from those sidelines, posed frontally the dynamic questions of mediation: in philosophy someone like Sorel, in politics Gramsci, or in cultural life, and through more round-about means, Walter Benjamin and Bertolt Brecht.

3. On a Few Hidden Precursors

It is apparent, then, that we have found our golden threads in the outlands and hard shoulders of the major doctrines, among the common stock of the apostles, litterateurs, strategists—men of expedients, henchmen, practitioners. Apostle is epistle: "*apos-tolès*," "*epistola*" have the same etymology. The apostle is the "letter" of the Holy Spirit, a proxy sender of the Almighty's messages. The apostles are better versed than their Messiahs in the "postal services and telecommunications" of the Truth because they are better placed for knowing that a brief epistle read by those it is addressed to will accomplish more for the Spirit than a Treaty or Summa kept in an *armoire*. This common sense may be the least commonly shared thing there is.[8]

Jesus functions as the sole Mediator of salvation but Saint Paul is the best on-the-job mediologist of Christianity. As was Lenin for Marxism. If one understands by *ideologue* the producer of a system for interpreting the real, which determines the objectives of collective action, and by *strategist* the organizer of the forces available for pursuing this action, which ensures how it is to be conducted in the field, the strategists have so to speak mediology as part of their very take or hold on life—as an instinct, not just a scientific competence.

---

[8] Above all among professional writers. I have spent time with a good number who considered the labor of the idea a fait accompli once they had put the finishing touches on the explanatory opuscule, the author's Society editorial project, or the book-that-definitively-resolves-the-question, confident in the *omne bonum est diffusum sui* of tradition (they position themselves rather to the Left). One recognizes others, on the opposing shore, who are so concerned with diffusion, editing, mailing, and marketing, that the content of the message matters little to them. On my left, good epistle-writers without any postal workers; on my right, trusty postmen carrying empty envelopes: the bringing together in real space and time of a letter *and* stamped envelope falls under the heading of a real exploit.

Instinctual mediology has existed in a practical form for centuries, in suspension with a thousand authors and actors of our
own history. Those who govern are more savvy about it than
those who are governed, for it applies to their very survival. As far
as thoughtful reflection about it is concerned, that is, a locally
reflected mediology in its raw state, one can say that its traces
become abundant beginning with the eighteenth century. We have
already seen why: up until that time epistemology was ruled by the
metaphysics of Light. It is with the Enlightenment [*Lumières* in the
plural], with the birth of a public opinion and civil society, that the
means said to be of vulgarization or more open disclosure also
become worthy of being given consideration. Human souls reeling
from the changes of this era and their beliefs shaken to their foundation: periods of instability or historical destabilization like this
are always more propitious for the deployment and thus closer
examination of symbolic tools than periods of order or consoli-
dation. The power of words is heightened in stormy times, and a
pre-revolutionary and revolutionary milieu is distinguished by a
mounting conductivity of ideas. Napoleon's remark that "Three
newspapers on the side of the opposition are more to be feared
than a thousand bayonets" was not thinkable coming from Louis
XV. In France the mediological intuition dwelled within men of
power well before men of learning began to be concerned with it.
And even then, it cannot be explained in the case of thinkers but
first in that of professional writers (historians, essayists, critics,
novelists, poets). Here, direct observation from experience has
had a lead of at least two centuries over speculation.

One would have little trouble culling indications of a mediological interest out of Michelet, when he sets the written culture of
the Girondins against the oral culture of the Montagnards. Nor
out of Tocqueville, from whom whole chapters might be taken,
like the famous one titled "How towards the middle of the eighteenth century men of letters took the lead in politics and the
consequences of this new development."* But it is the jolt of recognition I received reading Augustin Cochin's *Les Sociétés de pensée*

---

*This is the title of the first chapter in Part Three of Tocqueville's *The Old Regime
and the French Revolution*, English translation by Stuart Gilbert (Garden City:
Doubleday & Co., 1955), pp. 138–48. [Trs.]

et la démocratie and above all *La Révolution et la libre-pensée* (1924) which convinced me that an approach we might call cynical, or pragmatic toward social ideas, could be fruitful, and that it would be interesting to systematize it well beyond the historical juncture of the Jacobin episode. By reducing revolutionary ideas to their instrumental function Cochin wants to see in them nothing more than simple support structures for groupings of individuals by their affinities, against nature and without precedent (clubs, societies, spheres of influence, etc.). Capturing thought or philosophy in the snares of its own means of transmission, he discovers that what seems to be the truth of doctrine is found in its method of socialization and not its utterances. Diachronic examination of the logistical succession of steps of transmitting the message replaces the synchronic investigation of the order of reasons (the system of notions belonging to Jacobin ideology). Beneath the reductive method of the counter-revolutionary polemicist, it seems to me that we can detect the outlines of an intellectual revolution capable of transforming one day "the history of ideologies" into an annex of the history of techniques of organization. Forty years before "the medium is the message," someone claimed that "the method engenders the doctrine" and was not understood.

It is in the eighteenth century that there comes into being a breed of authors who are not yet journalists but are forced to busy themselves with what it means to make a book, to compose it, get it into print, sell it, live from it. There are men of letters who head toward (whether or not from a directly interested business angle) the literal manufacture of the letter—the papermaking industry, foundry casting and the print trade—who are concerned as professionals with the business of the book trade, with literary property and copyright infringement or the pirating of copies. There are writers for whom the written text as an objective *thing* is worthy of inquiry as both an object of curiosity and something at stake in relations of power. And there are professional publicists paid to know all too well that in matters of opinion just publishing is itself not the same as promulgating. This is why I cited Diderot in *Teachers, Writers, Celebrities* as mediology's great-uncle, and Balzac as its founding father. The genealogy exaggerates of course the literary aspect of mediations, but the two of them explored the three sides—political, technological, and cultural—of the mediological triangle. The essential correlation of the three poles did not escape the notice of these honorable ancestors: powers of opinion over governments, networks of circulation of the sign, and the typology of the literary milieu.

But it was the poets who pushed furthest the incursion. With poets it is as if one were dealing with less of the arbitrary and more of the pertinent; as if, being more attentive to the manners and matters of the act of saying (be it in sonorous vocality or graphic form), they had known before all the others (and dispensed as they are from the prejudices of meaning) how to disclose, to themselves and to us, *the sensoriness of signs and the variations of this sensoriness*. Too bad for us if this ascendancy detracts from the scientific credit—and if it came about that a poetics degraded into a doctrine came in for denunciation. We might think of Victor Hugo, whose "This will Destroy That, the Book will Destroy the Building" is not of course a compendium of mediology but a kind of obligatory "introit" preceding the mass that virtually introduces the concepts later labeled *milieu* and *medium*. Or of Baudelaire, who is at once alarmed and fascinated by the eruption of Niepce's invention in the midst of Gutenberg's. Or of Apollinaire, who measures by instinct the breaks with the past brought on by radio and film. And Breton, along with the Dadaists before him, who pick up on photography and give it a new twist, taking the medium in all the best and worst directions. I would also readily include in this list a great prose poet, eccentric and inspired: McLuhan, with whom I would associate (as far as images are concerned) that other poet of visual thinking, Serge Daney.

McLuhan is no theoretician or even a reasoner. He is on the model of Blake, a specialist and perhaps heir of Joyce and John Donne, bursting with penetrating and incoherent intuitions, a popular *vates* badly served by his theoretical speculation but carried along nevertheless, mediatically speaking, by his publicitarian aggressiveness. From the poetic side he has the virtue of attending to ambient conditions and all the variants of popular culture that are ordinarily scorned by professors. He proceeds by means of collages, short-circuits, and abrupt changes of subject, using ideas badly assimilated (but his own strange writings were no less so to the author himself). His guiding idea that form is content and medium message—is this not a poet's idea, or rather itself the form taken by the poetic work we can say he applied to the cultural forms of his time? Structuralism did not after all invent the notion of "structure": McLuhan put it to the test only to extend much further its rigors. Mediology did not invent "medium is message," to which it prefers, besides, the deeper less known aphorism of Cochin ("method engenders doctrine"). It prefers only to make these formulations exemplary of something that can be investigated systematically and align them with the more serious consistencies of a theory. Hence a certain ambivalence toward this illuminating visionary-crank, this improbable monomaniac in the same degree superficial and powerful. With McLuhan one must tirelessly peel away the husk of manic inspiration and carefully validate the kernel of truth.

Paul Valéry, that materialist of the abstract, was a kind of discrete and rigorous McLuhan. His subtlety and sense of the exact protected him from popularity. His operating definition of Mind as "power of transformation," and the intuition (on which he meditated for countless hours) that machines modify the conditions and nature of thought, make of this poet-philosopher one of the principal pioneers. Even if the mediologic reputation he deserves is not something widely recognized, we owe as much if not more to this agnostic as to the famed Catholic of Toronto. Another name stands out by its imposing presence: that of Walter Benjamin, an omnipresent adoptive godfather of mediology, with his dual allegiance to mysticism and technology (yet refraining intelligently from taking one for the other). "The Work of Art in an Age of Mechanical Reproduction" (1936) is one of our classics. Just as is, on the philosophical plane, Jacques Derrida's *Of Grammatology*, which offers a theoretical matrix for any applied mediology. As to the role played throughout the entire course of this crystalization by Michel Serres, the author of *Hermes* and *La Légende des Anges*, we concede that his presence on the examining committee does not facilitate here the exegesis.

The *bricoleur*, says Lévi-Strauss, works with signs and the engineer with concepts. The objection will be raised that one does not become an engineer by making do with and piecing together implements and equipment already to be found on board.

Collecting fragments from writings that prefigured mediological inquiry, the scattered materials of construction, is one thing; actually making a machine work according to plan is another. Mediology may still be a confederation of straggly residues, a precarious coalition of heterogeneous disciplines, and thus only an art of accommodating remainders or a meticulous *bricolage* to the second power. The threshold of a genuine task of engineering remains before it. At the least, the few works I have just cited make possible, along with others, an opening toward the unity of the concept, above and beyond a simple note-taking survey of some singled-out experimentations. I well suspect that if the abstract concept aims at being perfectly transparent to the reality it designates, it will never have (because of its diaphanous character) "the thickness of humanity" and the warmth of lived experience proper to full-blown empiricism (and which gives in return to the labors of *hommes de lettres* an incomparably "truer" charm). By these lights a system of notions will always be outdone by the bric-à-brac of "things seen."

4. One Path Like Any Other

"Every discourse on method," said Bachelard, "is a discourse of circumstance." Allow me then, honoring this truth, to recall what my own circumstances were like. For there was after all the simple order of an individual existence on the near side of these bookish discoveries made in such disorder. I was initiated into my studies of mediology unbeknownst to me, thrust into adulthood sometime during the sixties. The canonical question of the history of ideas—"do books make revolutions?"—is not only a question for the seminar room. For some people this was a question lived out over a long course—about ten years in my case. The majority of my fellow Normaliens (philosophers *and* militants) had summoned the wisdom to undertake head-on, but along distinct parallel tracks, revolutionary militancy and intellectual labor. I made the (philosophical) mistake of looking for ways to make the two converge, which led me toward leaving my country and *philosophia perennis* to try to make these opposites meet: saying and doing. The attempt was to bring about in Latin America a

certain kind of collective doing, an anonymous one emerging
from a certain kind of personal and authored saying (political
articles and booklets). It was the work of "agitprop" in a sense.
With the publicity given *Revolution in the Revolution?* which
was a question-marked, portable and succinct manifesto that theorized in 1966 the Cuban Revolution and called upon Latin
Americans to make other revolutions on the same model, I had
reluctantly become the apostle of an ephemeral and localized *-ism*:
focismo or the theory of the guerilla fire-pockets of rebellion.*
People have said that it was responsible for many deaths on Latin
American soil. I am not sure about the causal link, but can vouch
for occurrences of massacre as a direct and indirect witness. This
opuscule was distributed outside the continent, and translated
into many languages, enough to "act" or produce influence in
Turkey, Palestine, Thailand and elsewhere, as I discovered twenty
years later while travelling in these countries and happening upon
former political prisoners who would say to me "Hello, it was
your book that landed me in prison." Those who had had to stay
there would never have occasion to tell me this. It does present a
moral problem of responsibility, and a problem concerning the
nature of the justice system as well, since the codes that were in
force prescribed prison without parole for the "intellectual
authors" of "crimes." It was at all events a problem that, once the
first shocks and bumps in the road had been absorbed, I believed
I could add, by way of a modest contribution or brief illustration,
to the common store of studies led by the historian of long
chronology and wide scope: studies with titles like *The Origins of
Contemporary France* (Taine) or *The Intellectual Origins of the
French Revolution* (Mornet). And what of the question of causal
sequence from the Enlightenment to 1789? It is still being debated;

---

*Debray had espoused this strategy as a devotee of Ernesto (Che) Guevara
(1928–1967), the Argentinian medical student who became the principal architect of
domestic and foreign policy in revolutionary Cuba following the victory of Castro's
Rebel Army in 1959. Guevara had developed a theory of revolution, based on the
Cuban experience, whose revised Leninist tenets he exorted other Latin-American
revolutionaries to follow by taking up arms and forming roving bands of rural gueril-
las. The theory was known as *foquismo* from the guerilla group, the *foco*. Debray's
book was translated into English as *Revolution in the Revolution? Armed Struggle
and Political Struggle in Latin America*, tr. Bobbye Ortiz (New York: Grove Press,
1967; repr. Greenwood Press, 1980). [Trs.]

Roger Chartier has recently revived it with his *Cultural Origins of the French Revolution*. I do not know what place the minute sequence of "scholarly opuscule to militant military school" can occupy in the unfolding of this vaster history. But conscience without science being the soul's ruination, I at least told myself then, in consulting the glorious preceding events, that my minor misfortunes might be useful for something.

It was no real abandonment of the ground I was used to when, a few years later and in a French parliamentarian and legal context, I again took up the role of publicist, but still at the meeting point of the theoretical and practical spheres. Preaching in France for the political good cause, which was for me in the seventies something called the "Union of the Left"; composing a *Letter to French Communists*; apostolically getting involved in innumerable "interventions" both oral and written in order to bring about more quickly the conversions of peoples' sympathies—this modest social-democratic proselytism was in the end no less that of a mediator of utopias, a courier of programs. In short, it was the standard practice of the very model or carbon copy of a French intellectual confronted with an ideological message in the process of becoming a material force (or a weakness, which is the same operation assessed from the other direction). Here again it was not professionally uninteresting to follow the course of a discourse, the ground it had covered from its beginning to its falling-off point; and whether the particular issue might have been left-wing or right-wing is not of importance to the protocol of experience. This was what might be concluded from my experiment of participating, for example, in drawing up a *Charter of Freedoms* in 1978 under the aegis of Robert Badinter, and three years after that, in turning it into a piece of legislation, or into something resembling action (it is hard to say). The mysterious transition from saying to doing can be subjected to a banal, tried-and-true, as well as trying, test applicable to those who craft messages of collective interest: the translation of the space of their private apartments into that of state-owned historic buildings, parallel with the internal transformation of the culture of opposition into a culture of government. Being an adviser to princes betrays perhaps the vocation of philosophy—something that has been disputed since Plato—but surely not the cause of mediology. To produce discourses in places where decisions are made, a workaholic or an acolyte's job, is not the worst way to study the relations unifying the government of men with the administration of signs. Or perhaps what should have been said in this instance, the government of signs and administration of men.

What is generally called "being in power" is covered with opprobrium, though power is but a site of maximal powerlessness. This cannot hide from us the fact that it is also one among various trials for truth, the *experimentum crucis* of men of letters, the place where one is asked to pay in hard cash. It is also a site of strong news about the external world, which lowers (without canceling of course) the "ideological" coefficient of the contents. The pen pusher or scribe anxious to lessen the gap between what he can have learned about the state of the world and his own compatriots' state of mind conducts a *second* mediological experiment: one measuring a milieu's resistances of a quasi-physical nature vis-à-vis ideas that contradict his beliefs. Informed as I was at that time of strategic and diplomatic questions (by notes, telegrams, reports and travels), I was able to assess the relations of force between blocs, civilizations and countries and measure the full weight of symbolic panoplies, images, sounds, and myths—factors that are more and more decisive and always underestimated. I noted for example in 1984, having returned from Central Europe, that "there is more power in rock music, videos, blue jeans, fast food, information networks, and television satellites than in the whole Red Army." However the things I was able to publish on these subjects (*La Puissance et les rêves*, *Les Empires contre l'Europe*, *Tous Azimuts*) had just about zero resonance. I sought to explain in 1985, making use of supporting facts and statistics and contrary to the prevailing opinion at that time that the free world was encircled and infiltrated by the totalitarian menace, "that the democracies are doing increasingly well while the Soviet Union and its empire are a power in decline" (fourth quotation on the cover jacket of *Les Empires contre l'Europe*). But I was able to notice that my "message was not getting across," and that the most appreciated authors of the moment whom everyone was reading, quoting, and reviewing were those who were taking as their themes "the end of the democracies," "the Finland syndrome," "the immutable nature of the U.S.S.R." or the petrification of the societies of the East into a "statocracy." I could well extrapolate the same comparative game to other subjects connected with the international relations I was able to follow quite closely during a decade. It would confirm this hackneyed but instructive observation: the person who knows how to hang on to their reason cuts the figure of an oddball; the person who feeds collective delirium passes for being reasonable.

So the skepticism would be fooling itself that holds political judgments undecidable. There exists a simple and verifiable touchstone—aptitude for anticipating the event. Rereading magazines, newspapers and books ten years after their publication should be enough for deciding in these matters between the real and the unreal, for telling a certain historical clairvoyance from a simple ecological redundancy. It is especially in this sense that I became cognizant of the age-old dilemma of the reader or writer of public epistles to modern audiences: whenever his letters get the reality of things wrong by echoing all the ambient expectations, they have every likelihood of, in fact, reaching their addressees. When they get things right, that is to say, are displeasing, they will probably not even be read. Compare the social pulse-taking of Marx and August Comte—or the way the twentieth century has selected from between their two bodies of writings, identifying valid information in the one and rejecting the other as background noise. They offer another illustration of this curious phenomenon on the higher plane of great world visions. The mediologist with credentials for specialized study of qualitative phenomena may be a cynic, but not to the point of thinking that an idea, a system, a doctrine which does not "work" is on this account uninteresting or false (the sociologist Comte proved to have a prophetic pertinence, far superior to Marx). The proof would be a cutting edge in reverse: an idea that has impact on its environment over the short or medium run is quite probably a false idea. The antipathy of collectives to truth is no new discovery, but it does displace attention in a useful way from the message onto the milieu as a kind of "regional mail facility" of last resort. The term "influence" undoubtedly has the flaw of including within its figural texture what needs to be explained, but the man *without* influence is a mediological indicator of even more utility than the "man of influence." And the flop says as much about conditions of reception as the blockbuster. Having experienced these two conditions in succession is an almost scientific privilege. Given that no society is demystifiable (an effect of the theorem of incompleteness), it is normal that the mystifier should come across as more credible than the demystifier. But ample proof having been produced to show that "society runs on ideology like the car on gas" (Althusser), the moment comes when one is persuaded that being satisfied to pump gas has its limits, and that it's time to go about learning mechanics and opening up the hood to take a look at how the motor of belief really runs. The pump attendant is the *engagé* intellectual, the publicist always on the go, or the professional conference-frequenter and talker. The apprentice mechanic does not learn *rational* mechanical principles. To pass from activism to a possible pragmatics involves adopting a certain distance or disengagement. But the public speaking and other day-to-day interventions have fostered the long-term research on the phenomenon of intervening itself.

"Method," said Marcel Granet, "is the road once one has already traveled down it." May this felicitous formulation and avowal of modesty excuse the thesis defender for these few personal off-key notes—in an otherwise harmonious concert of objective reasons?

IV

Toward an Ecology of Cultures

1. Making Up for Delays

We would have liked in the final analysis to describe the dwelling places of thought, to tell the story of its relocations from place to place. From house to house, *oikos*. To proceed as if mediology could become in relation to semiology what ecology is to the biosphere. Cannot a "mediasphere" be treated like an ecosystem, formed on the one hand by populations of signs and on the other by a network of vectors and material bases for the signs? Cannot the object of the discipline, then, be defined in terms of the inter-actions between these two wholes? The different types or "species" of the world of symbols would no longer, from that point on, be considered in and for themselves, like isolated char-acters in a play who have stepped off the stage, but as part of the plots that weave them with their milieu and typical counterparts. What one would call the quantity of "semio-mass"—composed of two parts living and one dead—has of late dizzily rocketed within our social space, thanks to the new apparatuses of registering and storing traces. At such a moment, picking up the canoes for a dif-ferent kind of portage along dry ground would not be ill-timed when alternative routes are unnavigable. The "food chains" of the sign are being radically reorganized before our very eyes, the lev-els of cultural reproduction of knowledge are altering, and information is overloading and saturating the channels of its flow, putting on the agenda of survival a "dietetics of communication" (Joël de Rosnay's phrase). We might think of this latter as exer-cises of abstinence founded on a new criterion of pertinence.

Expecting that the coming compression of data through cable or wire cannot possibly be accompanied by an equivalent compression of the time needed to assimilate it, in the next century we will have periodically to sort through and prune the archive as well as intelligently rarefy or thin out consumption so as not to succumb. These developments are occurring as if the proliferation of symbols in the industrially developed North were already matching the demographic explosion in the planet's southern hemisphere. While the problems posed by rising population and industrialization are debated at the summits of industrial leaders and among inner circles of specialists, those posed by the proliferation of vectors of industrial concentration of signs and images are in earlier stages of scientific and political discussion. Though insights, analyses and proposals on these subjects continue to multiply, they remain filed under "miscellaneous," at the borderlines of the sciences and of more general legitimate concerns (the place where Goethe remarked that the professors "devour each other"). They remain in the unpaved shoulders of the road, so to speak, or in the margins of learned institutions. Will the rational scrutiny of the techno-cultural environment make up for its belatedness compared with the scientific exploration of the natural environment (at least as far back as Haeckel's ecology in 1866)?* We have no reason not to think so, even if what affects the inner time of human beings is less directly observable than what lays siege to their external space.

*Ernst Haeckel (1834–1919) is counted among the most influential disseminators of Darwin's ideas in Germany. Though much of his work now seems compromised in its monistic vitalism and importation into biology of the idealist strain of German nature-philosophy, he nevertheless made important contributions to classification, cell theory and embryology. Haeckel is perhaps most often cited for his systematic claims about recapitulationism, the "law" holding that ancestral adult stages of earlier organisms are repeated in the embryonic or juvenile stages of descendants. He argued notably that "Phylogenesis is the mechanical cause of ontogenesis" (from the *Anthropogenie*, 1874) (see especially Stephen Jay Gould, *Ontogeny and Phylogeny* [Cambridge: The Belknap Press of Harvard University Press, 1977], pp. 78–85). His work owes equal influence to the evolutionary theory of Goethe and Lamarck—to whom the book, identified with one founding moment of ecology, the *Generelle Morphologie* (1866), was jointly dedicated. In it "he combined Darwinism with elements from the theories of Lamarck and the nature-philosophers, stressing more than Darwin the doctrine of the inheritance of characteristics acquired under environmental influence . . . " (Stephen F. Mason, *A History of the Sciences*, rev. ed. [New York: Macmillan, 1962], p. 426). [Trs.]

An ecology *of cognition* is already well underway. It shows how the collective processes of knowing are guided as a function of the available equipmental systems [*appareillages*] (Pierre Lévy). It is without doubt the leading edge of a multifaceted mediology that would aim to encompass the whole of the symbolic milieu (ideologies and mythologies included), and in which a creative ecology of artistic acts would fully belong (my *History of the Western Eye* makes one among a hundred other contributions). Through its object as through its method, an "inter-discipline" can only be a discipline that synthesizes from other sources. Ecology too works in teams. It supposes indeed quite thorough specializations in genetics, agronomy, biology, thermodynamics, etc. Mediology, which supposes almost this many within the arc of the human sciences—sociologies, political sciences, semiology, varieties of history, the study of technology—will stand or fall on whether it can produce its work collectively. While at the same time seeking to redress the imbalances of excessive overspecialization to arrive at an overview of the relations between material base and symbols, it not only calls upon specialists of already constituted disciplines but welcomes the multiplication of both closely detailed and panoramic studies. Need we be more specific in saying that despite offerings of a certain terminological fecundity, we feel and know ourselves to be less competent for taking up the call of such an ambition than a worthy number of contemporary researchers whose names could be cited here and have been invoked so far?

Reversing the Goethean formulation, we may perhaps find it necessary to risk concluding that "what is on the outside is on the inside." Ambience-concepts like those of "mediasphere," "mediospace" or "mediorhythm" [see appendix] argue for a directional shift toward a reconsideration of milieus and climates more on the East-Asian model. Like any *relational* system of thought, sensitive to the distant harmonics of the *logocentrism* of the East (which the Japanologist and geographer Augustin Berque has explicated so deftly in his essays of "mesology" [from Greek *meso-*, "in the middle"]), mediology also turns its back on the logocentrism of our own localities. For the East has an edge over the West (or what was formerly considered its "belatedness" has actually saved it time). It is not its common practice to regard the subject as the measure of all things, emperor of his signs, master and proprietor of his culture: the stable, independent origin point around which (as for Westerners) turn things that are satellite-like, neutral, and inessential. Should not the "symbol-using animal" perhaps be approached *à la japonaise*, as the mobile "projection" of exterior and changing sites, and not as an "I" extracted from the rest of the game, overseeing it all from some regal balcony? Mediological man does not cohabitate with his technological surroundings, he is inhabited by his habitat; constructed by the niche he has constructed. The East-Asian model does not say "My body is mine, but I really *am* my body." Why can we not train ourselves, as Berque calls for us to do, to replace the sentiment that "I *have* an environment, it belongs to me" with "I *am* my environment"? I am not in front of, with or against, but within, with and through my environment of technology. I "am" my automobile, my telephone, C.N.N., Airbus and CD-ROM. I am the "inside" of this "outside": it may involve an inversion and excentering of consciousness that can doubtlessly be painful, but it can perhaps also be exhilarating like breaking and entering or computer hacking. I say this with all the discomfort that an episodic reader of the eminences of Husserl or Heidegger can experience hearing such theses that run as obviously counter as they do to our best ontologies. To truly "measure thinking by the yardstick of doing and producing," to "transform mind into an appendix of the body and of its instruments"—are not such notions sinfulness itself in the eyes of a philosophy of Being that rebels at the idea of a close and forceful inspection of our carriers of meaning?

It is only bumping against the sand that can teach fish about water. "Pain," Paul Valery observed, "is everything toward which one directs one's complete attention." One gives one's surroundings full attention when they are the setting of one's misfortune or illness, once the trouble has advanced quite far. In the same way that we think about our native language when the occasion demands we no longer speak it, or that we discover our own country in exile (nothing like expatriation to make a patriot). The figure of loss is an encumbrance that causes a coming to consciousness (ecological as well as mediological), and for the same reasons as expatriation. But has there ever been an owl of Minerva that wasn't a night flier? In the melancholy that is so natural to these crepuscular take-offs lies the danger of a certain sluggishness and slowing down, for the unhappy consciousness is gladsomely reactionary: it wants first of all to return home, and grasps the emerging medium only as the defigured version of the medium it renders obsolete. Plato, living at the cutting edge of the logosphere, puts its medium of writing on trial in the name of the preceding *mneumosphere* of unrecorded orality. He (or rather one of his doubles, the Egyptian king Thamus in the *Phaedrus*) sees only the failures of the invention when measured against the primordial orality: writing is going to make us forgetful souls, incapable of memory and thus of true knowledge; it will ruin the common striving toward truth supposed by dialectic and dialogue, all for a sad and monotonous solitude. At a time when the conditions that marked the graphosphere or print culture were in full sway, Rousseau favors the expressive over the printed word, yearns for the childhood of signs in which only basic human needs stand out in their harmony, and longs to rediscover behind representations the pure presence of festivals, countrysides, and human voices. And now today, others who are critics of the ways of the videosphere are seen as inconsolable purists of the lost order of Books. This bitterness sometimes can blunt the speculative joy of understanding. Some reasons however can also be found for excusing it. If it is true that the ecological study of the natural does not really come naturally, the ecology of the cultural is squarely *against* nature, so much are we biologically amnesiac, blindly narcissistic: for systems of mediation have the art of seeming *im*-mediate and transparent to active consciousness. The only time that a short-sighted person notices his glasses is when they are lost or broken. Likewise, when a regular reader of the Bible suddenly wonders to himself what language God spoke in creating the world with words—the Old Testament's authors having naturally neglected this small detail—he is not far from realizing that God does not exist. And this is something that can be "sometimes a real nuisance," as the Father remarks in Sartre's *Condemned of Altona*.

Originating as a science in the nineteenth century, ecology has in the twentieth inspired a social practice. Today it leads a double life, of the specialist and of the militant: it is at once a discipline and a cause, a theory and a politics. From its scientific object it has drawn objectives: to preserve the evolutionary potentialities of nature by safeguarding endangered species and natural habitats. Not content to describe the present and reconstitute the past, there are those among its practitioners who have every intention of predicting the future and preventing the worst. Side by side with the abstentionists who refuse to intervene by acting upon nature, are the managerial ecologists moved by the duty of interference to invent a paradoxical technology of the natural. Will mediology have one day to imitate them? That is, to complete an ecological ingeniousness (inspired and enabled by technology) with an engineering proper?

This would not mean superadding onto the rights of animate beings something like "the rights of machines" (whether or not obsolete ones), but rather reacculturating sites of memory that have in effect been declared disaster zones, traditions of craft and organizations of artisanship becoming extinct, just as we now "re-naturalize" certain set-aside areas.* Consider a letterpress printer's workshop using lead type in its distinctiveness as the locality of a culture, or a film editing room with its technicians.

---

*Debray's invocation of "sites of memory" (*lieux de mémoire*) can be linked with an ambitious study of symbols, "objects, instruments or institutions" of the French cultural *patrimoine* begun in 1984 under the editorial direction of Pierre Nora, *Les Lieux de mémoire* (Gallimard, "Bibliothèque des Histoires" series, 4 volumes). A collection of detailed historical case studies of institutions and topoi as varied as the glorification of the illustrious dead, naming streets, constructing genealogies, coronations, the *grande exposition*, the Collège de France, etc., this work attempts to selectively inventory the material culture, iconography and both literal and mental geography of traditions that have been endlessly rewritten as part of the history of representation and reinterpretation. Debray's call for a heightened "ecological" consciousness of the preservable value of outmoded symbolic practices, though it may partially overlap with a more properly national heritage of artifacts and rituals, seems here to be perhaps less overtly inscribed in the enduring political life of specifically French historical events, customs and memories than concerned with a generically Western history of media and technology, not without application to the ongoing globalization and modernization experienced by non-European countries as well. On this latter subject, much of the detailed work done so far studies the less recent history of technological development and is, as one would expect, highly critical of European technology's implication in imperialism. See for example Michael Adas, *Machines as the Measure of Men: Science, Technology, and Ideologies of Western Dominance* (Ithaca: Cornell University Press, 1989) and Eric R. Wolf, *Europe and the People without History* (Berkeley: University of California Press, 1982). [Trs.]

Are not such places as precious, and precarious, as a patch of green in a suburban district of concrete? Cannot colorization, or the heavy further editing of films that is done to accommodate interruptive television advertising, be likened, *mutatis mutandis*, to the pollutions or eyesores of a stretch of high-speed train track in the Provençal countryside, or a nuclear waste preprocessing plant? We speak about Earth Day. Why not tomorrow, no pleasantry intended, a day devoted to celebrating celluloid, vellum paper, or vinyl records? To Nagra, the professional use of tape recorders, the Steadicam, the portable camera, or the Rolleiflex?

Let us enlarge on these points a bit.

2. For a Media-Ethics

New capacities for intervening directly in the genesis of life, as a consequence of the qualitative surge in biotechnologies, have obliged all the developed countries to reflect seriously and collectively on this subject. The time may not be far off when the complex of moral, social, legal, and economic questions raised by our capacities for intervening in the genetic springs and flows of cultural forms—as a consequence of the unprecedented boom of technologies of transmission—will necessitate in its turn the definition of a *media-ethics*. This would clearly require an extension, here as elsewhere, of the problematic that welds together S.T.S. (Science, Technology, Society) to the level of S.T.P. (P. for politics). But under what conditions is a politics of technology possible? Under the precondition that one does not err on the side of undue anxiety. The worry that perceives the threat of *one* unified Technology to "the humanist tradition" is certainly not for the best. Pitting valiant soldiers of print culture against those new pioneers of the Screen who are all the rage is no mournful Quarrel of the Ancients and the Moderns. It is rather a quite ancient case of mutual mistaken identities.

The heated and recurring wrangles over "the relations between technology and culture," in fact, seem to be founded on the Aristotelian opposition between *Form*, which is taken to be solely active and individualizing, and *matter*, an infinitely malleable recipient. The two come together in the act of traditional handicraft (producing a crater or amphora). Setting up technology and culture as external to one another, though normal for the potter's reflex, issues in a false problem (as elsewhere in the case of the old antinomies of individual vs. society, or mind vs. body). The greatest portion of technological objects and the series of operations they undergird *are themselves vectors of culture*. Consider again the mechanical clock, that medieval invention at once political and spiritual in which Mumford saw "the most progressive machine of modern technology." It was as much an instrument for measuring time as a tool of monastic discipline and communal control—as the means for synchronizing mens' actions and establishing the rhythms of prayer. Our symbolic relation to the real has always been mediated by technical systems and mechanical assemblages, beginning with that highly polyvalent tool if ever there were one that is the human body. "We have committed the fundamental error," wrote Marcel Mauss in "The Technologies of the Body," "of only judging there to be technology when there is an instrument."* The anthropologist demonstrated (as has more than one historian following him) that "the body is man's first and most natural instrument," or, more exactly, that there is no "natural manner of being" for the adult person. The uses to which the body is put, its customs—even those that are the most individual and ordinary, like walking, swimming, posture at table, or the positions of the hands—are collective elaborations. Produced technologically by a cultural transmission (or culturally by a technological transmission), the human body is the first and foremost of our mixed machines: a living mediation of intersections between orders, artifact, and nature (separated by our mental dichotomies). It is here that these sectors alter one another as they intersect, because by coming into relation each of the linked terms is transformed.

We need to recognize that the actual devices of cultural or political production are regularly excluded from these productions themselves. Mind does not find it congenial to pay off the debts it owes matter, nor does interiority those it owes exteriority. The political sciences have for a long time been reluctant to gauge the

---

*See Marcel Mauss, "Les Techniques du corps," *Journal de Psychologie normale et pathologique*, 32 (1935), pp. 271–93. [Trs.]

invention of democracy by the instrumental media or prostheses [*appareillages*] of writing—that seemingly minor system of tablet-stylus-alphabet that was at the heart of the great Hellenic legislative tables, and thus of the monumental publicness of the laws, "applied to good and bad alike," without which Athenian public space could not have been constituted. As Marcel Detienne and others have pointed out, it is worth rising above the barriers of the traditional political philosophy perspective to recall that Solon the legislator was above all a law-writer, a legi-grapher; and that isonomy (democratic equality before the law) presupposes the inscription and making public of words. The complex cognitive activity of writing is by itself a technical instrument that can be assimilated, like the lever and the toothed gear, to a primary machine (in its canonical definition, "any instrument designed to transmit the action of a force onto a point that does not already lie in its direction, or to change the direction of this force").[1] Hittite cuneiform writing had produced those novel cultural objects: tables, lists, inventories, dating systems, etc. The vocalic alphabet, transmitted from Syrio-Phoenician to the Greek city-state, made possible not only the first government of men by men (and not by the gods or their prophets) but also an amazing space for displays of learnedness, which extended the rights of citizenship to the arts of argument, to a critical relation to tradition, and to the subjection of rumors and myths to new norms of veracity. Among the written products of literacy's spelling book an innovative proto-technology for storing the flowing tides of human thoughts—could be counted not only legislation, philosophy, and tragedy, but also the geometrical symbol, cartography of inhabited lands, and medical prognosis (Euclid, Anaximander, and Hippocrates).

Today's "humanists" would be quick to define culture as the entirety of those functions that offer resistance to technology, in the same way life resists death. They seem to forget that fated solidarity of design which inscribes man in machine at the very threshold of our humanities or liberal arts. Behind every collective subjectivity, one or several technical systems are at work, and vice versa. No more than the fact of technology exists as an ideal

---

[1] Tradition lists seven primary machines: lever, pulley, lathe or axle, gear, inclined plane, screw, and wedge.

autonomy does the fact of culture exist autonomously. Each controls the other. And with man manufacturing the tool that in turn manufactures its maker, the *machina ex homine* of the humanist fails to invalidate the *homo ex machina* of the anthropologist (of which the *homo politicus ex scriptura* would be another variation). Unquestionably, matter can move faster than mind; and the dynamics of technologies of the intellect widen the furrows between the inherited paradigms of earlier tools and the solicitations and demands of more recent machines. A person will therefore feel divided between the symbolic culture he receives from his history and the technological culture of the present moment, between what he calls values, on the one side, and norms, on the other. An uneasiness, confusion or "crisis" arises within us when automatisms of different ages become superimposed. We often sublimate this discrepancy of phases into a split (or more or less pathos) between cultural *values* and industrial *norms*—inasmuch as we call "value" a technological norm long ago internalized, buffed to a high gloss by use and absolved of its technicity by a millenarian legitimacy. The fact is that the legacy of semantics and speculation attaching to the techniques of writing (art, religion, philosophy, and ethics) cannot be brought into line with electronic and digitized systems. This deep, undeniable dissociation between yesterday's and today's inventions should instead be an incentive to "integrate technology into culture," as the consecrated expression would have it, rather than open the rift, or further lend it legitimacy, between the two. But whether this ultimate aim is valid or not, realistic or unattainable, one would do wrong to omit the fact that this integration has always been a reality from the standpoint of positive history. We call "culture" an incessantly renegotiated interaction between our values and our tools (and it is a halt in these negotiations that creates, as far as culture is concerned, "technological obscenity"). Culture would be understood then as the imprint of a mediasphere's mechanics when the obvious variety of collective personalities could no longer be explained while remaining at a single homogeneous stage of the history of technologies. With the same vegetable essences the human mind can make a Japanese garden or a garden of the French variety. Everyone knows that being "in itself" is a far cry from being "for itself," similar to the distance between the universal neutral space of the physicist and the highly singular locales of space as it is lived and perceived. A collective individuality, one might say, stands in the same relation to the predominant technological milieu-medium as the landscape in the form of a fact of sensibility stands to the environment as a physical fact: both entail the subjective interpretation of an objective material by a historically determined community. Such a ratio would be the equivalent for collective identity, if you will, of the gene-environment pair vis-à-vis the source of individual life.

3. Rehabilitating Technology

It may be that conceiving culture nowadays by starting from technology has become more productive than the converse. This properly medialogical gesture is not made without some risks, of course, but they seem to us less than those that arise from putting technology on trial as a denaturing, dehumanization, loss of authenticity, "arationality," and overlooking of Being. Without undertaking here a discussion of Heidegerrian *Gestell*, we note that the discourse of sin and the Fall, the latent matrix of most contemporary excommunications of the machine, enjoys a bountiful declension (spirit falling into matter, the immutable into becoming, immediacy into mediacy, the transcendental into the empirical, Being into temporal being, etc.). One is never far from setting up the comforting cushion of a notion, more or less ideal or fictive, of an original and originary man, at once immutable and faultless, something like a human nature that is buried away, lost, or insistent. Paleontology offers no confirmation here. We will not take up in detail here Leroi-Gourhan's demonstrations of the *co-evolution* of the cortex and silex, or rather of the reciprocal process of *homo sapiens'* cortical and technological development ("tool for the hand and language for the face are the two poles of a single system").* This suggests the conclusion that technology—

---

*André Leroi-Gourhan's *Le Geste et la parole* has been translated into English by Anna Bostock Berger as *Gesture and Speech*, intro. Randall White (Cambridge: The MIT Press, 1993). Bruno Latour also takes up this motif of *Homo faber fabricatus* in his "On Technical Mediation—Philosophy, Sociology, Genealogy," *Common Knowledge*, vol. 4, no. 1 (Spring 1995), pp. 29–64. [Trs.]

the pursuit of life by other means—served as a motive force behind the breakthrough of hominization, a key to the zoological switch-over. While the animal remains genetically programmed by and stuck to an organic code that is fixed and specialized, human ethnicity breaks away from the specificity of *biological* memories. This is owing to a continual movement of individual faculties in and through those organic "organs" that are at first tools, then machines, then entire technologies (memory and computation themselves becoming "excorporated" today in artificial intelligence). "Ethnic evolution turns humanity into an externalized body whose global properties are in a state of accelerated transformation." One feels justified in denouncing the tyranny of technological mediations from the moment one believes, as Rousseau did, that every externalization denatures, that every transcription is tantamount to a lie, every representation amounts to defiguration—hindering expression from coinciding with what is expressed; appearance with being; the trace, with the thing. Yet observations by this same prehistorian discover in the "ex-corpo-realizing" of man's most intimate nature the very signature of humanity. He sees and documents that "the human group behaves in nature like a living organism," assimilating (to survive) his material surroundings both vegetable and animal through the intermediary of a membrane of artifacts (able to consume his woods thanks to the adze, his meat by means of the arrow, knife and pot, etc.). Citing such examples, should he not instead single out for praise our recourse to tools and our rescue by mediations? Technology is just as much our fate as it is our fortune. It is an anti-fate and a redressed infirmity, as the myth of Protagoras had foreseen with great exactitude—a myth that translated in its own way the human being's biological lack of finish (the young of *homo sapiens* being the most premature at birth of all mammals). When Prometheus steals fire from the gods and offers technical ingenuity to humans, it is not by pride or for pleasure but for want of anything better and through sheer necessity. He must make reparations for the neglectfulness of his brother Epimetheus, the absent-minded god who having provided all the animals with specific attributes suited to their survival, had nothing left to distribute to the last little one of the lot, man, left completely naked and condemned to die of his feebleness. The nature of man being unique in the animal kingdom because it was to have no nature, he could do nothing but ask of technological genesis what his zoological status had refused him at the outset. He thus turned around, by his own doing, a deficiency of being to a specific advantage. The *faber* created the *sapiens*; the external, the internal. Technology can be understood to have invented culture and man himself, from which follows the need not to say "the machine today replaces man," but "yesterday's man for a long time made up for a provisional shortcoming in his machines with personal, physical and intellectual interventions that are from now on partially rectified by artificial intelligence." The process of hominization, in going about its business, is presently passing from physical work to logical work, from motor to computer or muscle to synapses. Nothing that astonishing here, even if our machines are gaining in importance what they lose in volume.

To all this one may still reply, not unreasonably, that culture can be defined as that which cannot be externalized technologically, nor mechanized, nor perhaps even objectified. An inorganic mechanical-electron organ can be endowed with logical capacities, relieving us of fastidious tasks; but the combinations of symbolic units, a subject-less process, allows one to manipulate syntaxes but not to interpret situations in the semantic sense. Can there be an "artificial culture" as there is an "artificial intelligence," if in fact "culture" means the implicit and ambiguous—and also dream, art, feelings, meaning and value? Our robotic machines have acquired sight, hearing and touch (for recognizing forms and playing checkers, for instance), but we well know, or have the suspicion, that thought is not the same thing as calculation, nor the brain as intellect (the encephalitically reptilian or rhynchocephalian part of our nature waiting to come out), and that a consciousness is made in a different way from the most impressively performative machines of cognition. Culture surveys and encircles acts of knowledge, as life itself looks out over and includes cultural activities. Yesterday the machine could stand as a model for how the body could be questioned and conceptualized (Descartes); and today, with the computer, for how we can question and conceptualize intelligence (Turing). But it will never be able to serve as a model for thought's thoughts about itself—for the final reason that a machine is not mortal and only a mortal being can attain the symbolic universe of values and meanings. Death as well, both anticipated and deferred by technology's take on the world, is an impregnable reserve of human beings. Consciousness of mortality, the motor of our technologies' dynamism and rapidity of movement, remains surely the irreducible inner space of the human.[2]

To give up thinking of the transmission of ideas as a translation of idealities across an inert and neutral technologic ether, for the Western mindset, is to consent to an undeniable deprivation of its sense of entitlement. The teacher for example knows, however, that neither the same knowledge, nor chiefly the same idea of what knowledge is, is not transmitted intact. And this is even more so the case depending on whether the classroom tools are chalk and chalkboard, overhead projector, or computer. Like the nature of civic values, the contents of bodies of learning are not indifferent to the mechanisms of transmission and the methods they bring about. As Wittgenstein put it, "one cannot give someone measles over the telephone." We would add: nor can the law of gravity, along with the method of analysis on which its construction depends, be taught using the audiovisual of a dropping apple. The "technologies of intelligence" are unquestionably less "pliable" and transparent than their users would like to think—persuaded by their instinct and tradition, as we all are, that the subject is sovereign over its medium, like Michelangelo's Idea over the Carrara marble. The tool's neutrality as a passive thing subjected to the neat finalities of a soul that puts it to use is a notion that goes back to Aristotle, and, via another angle of approach, to Descartes. One might look there for the sources of this instrumental conception of the instrument, this utilitarian vision of the tool. These are attractively artless tautologies, yet fallacious ones reliant on a certain humanist reflection on media as simple means. This speculative illusion (if illusion it be) has in other applications had some highly visible and positive

---

[2] I refer on this issue to the fundamental reflection of Bernard Stiegler, and especially to his thesis *La Faute d'Epiméthée. La Technique et le temps* (under the direction of Jacques Derrida) (Paris: Galilée, 1994).

ramifications, on a moral and political plane, in that it submits that no single technology is good or bad in itself.[3]

Objective knowledge has been advancing for centuries now under a series of shocks that periodically wound human narcissism (Copernicus, Darwin, Freud), though it is certainly not sufficient to humiliate the human spirit in its illusions of sovereignty to gain a truth. All the same, if we think and act *in* our instruments and not only by and with them, if a message's efficacy is not inherent to it but the factor of a certain milieu of transmission or mediasphere, we can no longer represent man at the center of his environment like a captain in his ship. Neither outside nor peripheral, the term "milieu" no longer refers to an encircling ring of more or less influential circumstances surrounding a fixed center of reference, in accordance with the mechanists' model of the eighteenth century, or equally to what lies between two centers or to a simple vehicle of action (Canguilhem). The milieu becomes itself a motor or proto-motor of energetic symbolisms. If my instruments do not have the same ideas that I and my ideology have (which may be true on another plane for the unconscious as well), and if it is compulsory that I give up on the latter by going through the former, will it not be my technological milieu whispering my ideas in my ear? What then remains of the individual actor-enunciator-programmer? And of the mind's sovereignty, if it in fact "is only of account by virtue of the mediations it engenders and through which it passes" (Dagognet)?

The predominant question is what part of the moral subject's hold over his technological medium endures when that medium follows its own evolutionary constraints. Simondon and Leroi-Gourhan, each in his own way, have taught us to acknowledge two important realities: the one, "the organizing dynamism of

---

[3] One such historical effect of this way of thinking was a certain enlightened stoicism when facing military setbacks. In 1940, we find de Gaulle maintaining that France has lost a battle simply in terms of mechanics, and that this defeat has no moral meaning. Pétain is the one who moralizes, seeing in the inferiority of the French armed forces a punishment, a pretext to repent in expiation. Convinced of the axiological neutrality of the materials involved and more generally of the sheer mechanics at work, de Gaulle holds to the simple and forceful idea that one must eventually obtain for oneself the material means of a material superiority, and that's all there is to it.

objects' developmental lines of descent"; the other, the quasi-biological and assuredly universal tendency that pushes the silex flint stone held in the hand to acquire a handle, the bundle dragged along on two poles to become equipped with wheels, the wheel to lead to a wheel brace, and this latter, in its turn, to suggest the need for a transmission belt. All human groups, independently of their ethnic determinations, have resolved the problem of obtaining wood through the adze, fire through the forge, what to do with thread through the spindle, and of roofing through the A-frame's slanted sides. These resolutions have come about with the same necessity that shapes the fusiform profile on organisms who move through water; the morphology of a boat, on whales; and the spiral shell, on gastropods. Just as animal species follow a "blueprint" permitting more effective contact with their specific habitat, so do techno-cultural objects obey their genetic logic. Even if the universal tendency can, for each function, give rise to differently formed objects (witness the thousand forms taken by sabers and knives for cutting through solids), like a ray of light refracting differently through a different lens, convergence eventually imposes itself. Objects over time gravitate toward their perfection. And in much the same way that there is no regression of the living being (but a growing complexity of genetic combinations), technological development is condemned to progress. Political regimes have been observed to regress from democracy to dictatorship, but you will not find a farmer turning in his tractor for a plow, nor his plow for a hoe. Nor a city dweller swapping his portable transistor for an old-style crystal radio set, or a color television for black and white. And certainly not a soldier exchanging machine gun for crossbow; or a doctor, antibiotic for home remedy. But any philosopher who passes from Wittgenstein to Parmenides will not be accused of regressing. It is a distinct privilege to profess no knowledge of the law of permanent innovation prompting a "going ever forward." But the anti-progressive running in place that is traditionally sanctioned and indeed recommended in the case of the arts, religion, philosophy, literature, is not invoked for technology. We have no hold, it seems, on a techno-scientific process of becoming that is ever-accelerated (by the increasingly close union of research and development)—a process that for its part does have a hold over us: and a vexing dissymmetry this is (for the pride of a monarchical subject).

4. Ethics Under Pressure

Under these conditions, which are rather humbling when all is said and done, how is it possible to lay out some sort of room for a kind of freedom? How can the mind avoid becoming the tool of its tools? Perhaps by taking them more seriously than, heretofore, a certain speculative disdain has managed to do. It could well be that a *humanist practice*, as it turns out, passes through the stage of refusing every *theoretical humanism*. This means granting mechanical systems more (autonomy) while *ceding them less* (fewer powers). This wished-for reciprocity, assuming the partners of equal and respectable strength, will seem paradoxical. Let us recall the inverse paradox that resulted from the triumphalist illusion and technological indifference of the attitude expressed by us on the Left that "television will be what we make of it": to bend to the medium's commands was to become undone, morally and politically. The manipulator manipulated by his own apparatus rehearsed a scene of less humorousness than Louis Lumière's watered watering-can-wielder. A clear-headed assessment of the objective properties of technical systems and media apparatus, by political leaders and others in charge, would do less harm to the capacity or potential of political action than to political *illusion*, i.e. the assumption that "if our politics are good, all the rest will follow." In this latter view, it is as if the medium were merely a matter of stewardship, and television a bicycle. Or as if a machine could be changed by decree. A good politics can no more prevent a mass medium from functioning according to its own economy than it can prevent a severe drought. The primacy of a moral willfulness or resolve over a given generation of technological systems has never gone the length of intellectually devaluing those systems. And "assuring the integrity or security of things of the spirit" was not the same as sheltering them from their machines. It makes little sense to de-mechanize culture; but to de-sanctify *technè*, does. By sanctifying nature, the Greeks forbade intervening in it technologically, making artifice a sacrilege.

By excessively regarding technology as sacred (no longer its immutability but its upheavals and turning points), one would soon give up dialoguing with it freely. Facing the universe of technology, human unsubmissiveness and intellectual generosity will increase and decrease together. All of which supposes something like a third-alternative critical stance between the apocalyptic and apologetic tones, between the classical humanities' "nothing essential can be technological" and the latest futurisms' "everything is essentially a technical question." It would hold out some promise of a cautionary discernment attentive to the ambiguities and potentialities of our devices and systems.

There is a bio-ethics because in this area we know how (more or less) to distinguish the good, namely respect for life and freedom of choice, from the bad. Preventing illness, prolonging life, relieving suffering are at least uncomplicated desiderata, for a curative or prognostic medicine. The sciences of life can find themselves in agreement in defining their objects: health, the pathological, individual identity, death. The sciences of culture have a long road to travel if they are to isolate consensuses equivalent to these, and it will take time to define the ends that a cultural ecology would be able to set for itself. At the heart of both these inquiries, the stakes are no less grave. We are aware that a manipulation of embryos or *in vitro* fertilization has something to do with the integrity of the human person, and, one thing leading to another, with the genetic legacy of the species. We surmise that the inclusive and invasive networks of broadcasting, circulation, and distribution [*diffusion*] (or, in the case of film, the monopolistic temptation of the Hollywood model) are immediately relevant to certain potentials of creativity, the survival of indispensable specialized professions, and the cultural legacy of entire communities. These power technologies whose form the culture industries take *in addition*, centered as they are on the logistics of dispensing imagistic imagination and knowledge, just as the bio-industries are centered on living processes, carry norms along with them. But the new technologies of images, sounds, and signs do more than modify the norms that sway audiences, influence consumption, and control the recording and storage of traces, data bases, and memories.

They tend to globalize one sole political economy of videospheric consciousness that risks fostering harsh conditions for those who deviate from or disturb its status quo. The sense that the living, procreative and mortal human subject has been transformed into an object of technological manipulations has visibly mobilized a sense of social responsibility. The transformation of the *cultural* human subject (in its decision-making, desiring, imaginative and emotional life) into an object of manipulations of the same order has not yet openly mobilized a corresponding *responsibility* in the minds of actors as in those of the decision-makers. Or at least not beyond a minimal working code of moral obligations or deontology among journalists on the one hand, and, on the other, a legislative framework improvised without regulating ideas over the long term (even if it is of course never a bad idea in the short term to regulate, for example, photo-copying, since reproduction can destroy production). Genetic manipulations alarm us to the point where it seems natural to pass laws; mediatic manipulations produce little more than a smile, and regulation here seems against nature. It is as though the sacredness of the human genome, on the biological plane, were eclipsing collective things that might be held sacred but that appear more diffuse and uncertain, on the historical plane.

In the evolution of species as of cultures, life is synonymous with divergences from the norm: it produces differences. Yet even as it loosens the constraints of our *natural* options and multiplies human masteries over the world, technology brings with it standardization: it reduces differences by a common dialect of unifying norms that make possible wide communication, compatibility and exchange, while also trivializing (or canalizing) them. Whether from sun, water, wind, or atom, all these energy sources are transformed when emerging from turbines into a general and uniform equivalency: the kilowatt-hour. Man's techno-cultural invention is inscribed in a dialectic between variation and the norm, between a worldwide lingua franca and local idioms. The dialectic has no end, fortunately. To preclude it from finishing would be precisely a plausible goal of a carefully thought-out action of the powers that be (an action that the partisans of a general furtherance of entropy in these matters will not fail to judge coercive or bureaucratic). The play of life, on the contrary, is what needs preserving, in its free movement of differentiation. We cannot greet as a bad piece of news, in this respect, the fact that corresponding to the omnipresent and omnivorous technological megasystem there has been no appearance of a planetary megaethnicity—as Leroi-Gourhan himself had, we believe mistakenly, foreseen (in 1965). The hypothesis he put forward of the ethnic organization of populations falling into obsolescence does not seem to be coming true. The standardization of technological norms and modes of life, on the planetary scale, is not being answered by a corresponding uniformity of collective dreams and religions. The abolition of delays and distances of communication between groups in the global village does not erase all borders and mix together peoples' hearts into one. Quite to the contrary, the material unity of our mechanical devisings seems to revivify the ethno-cultural divisiveness of dispositions. It's as if far from being diluted in the standardization of goods and services, local memories drew back inward and hardened, to the point where they shattered federations and empires to bits. As if culture as a given fact diverged further in proportion to the convergences of technology as a given fact. This acquisition of greater similarities draws people so far apart that a deliberate movement in the opposite direction—from the closed to the open—could soon become necessary. The ecumenism of interconnected networks (air transportation, telecommunications, broadcasting networks, electronic mail, virtual communities, etc.) is not a phenomenon composed exclusively of positive factors. But it is a fact that it opens up enclaves of isolation, de-stabilizes parochially communitarian domination, ventilates refuges musty and stagnant with traditions—and liberates in this sense singular energies that have been put to sleep or imprisoned. The two moments (one a systolic contraction, the other a diastolic dilation) are to be combined; and a "respiratory" alternation of this kind calls for a certain regulation of technological systems that would be specifically political in nature. The de-coupling of different frames of reference to space and time between one worldwide economic environment whose evolution is precipitate, and numerous territorialized ethnic milieus whose evolution is sluggish, creates a situation of dire urgency. An international advisory committee or, at the national level, a pluridisciplinary

watchdog or observatory, would have more than enough to keep
it busy. Indeed, without an informed and concerted voluntarism,
the present laissez-faire in this area will produce the recoil effect
of nationalistic or denominational closures. *Bio-diversity* in
nature has become a shared concern. In the cultural sphere, the
sustaining of a *medio-diversity* will have to be negotiated in its
finer points with the media's erosion of difference and the same
homogenization of content that is reflected in the technical networks of diffusion. This is something that assumes fine
navigation between an excess and a dearth of competition and
openness. Narrow is the gate, and the wisdom of nations alone
will not be enough for the passage through (no more than the
body's wisdom amounts to a science of dietetics).

We should take care, meanwhile, that the cult of the new does
not simply come to replace among young minds the old cult of
force. It would not be an undue diminution of innovation into a
derisive "gadget" or "thingamajig" if we adopt toward it a certain civic and critical vigilance. This latter is a must for numerous
reasons. The control we can acquire of an innovative system, as
it is by no means given, remains unstable, reversible, subject to
down times. No tool is fully neutral, infallible, or without its
conveniences inducing passivity in its users. An advance in technology can accompany or favor a social or cultural regression.
There is no instance of people made freer by technological
change that does not pay for itself with a certain degree of subjection to the enfranchising system. (As a concrete illustration:
the high-speed rail line between Paris and Lyons that does so
much to increase exchanges between the two metropolises accel-
erates the deterioration of the rural fabric stretching between
the line's terminal points.) But vigilance is mainly grounded in
principle, for there is every advantage to be gained by establishing a proper proportion of relative strengths vis-à-vis our
prostheses. Absolutizing or fetishizing them would limit our abil-
ities to truly make them our own as a function of our properties
and purposes. One could say apropos the technological object
that the set-up is slavish but the use free, relatively. Unlike the
genetically programmed animal, "man *can* bring many solutions
to a given problem posed by the environment." The *reflective*
relation to a set of tools or equipment is not the same as the

instinctive relation to a natural stimulus insofar as man is not fated to fall automatically and humbly into mechanical provocation. As a rule, life led by a living being that is fully "remote-controlled" by its environment is life about to perish. A culture programmed by its technological medium of existence would be by that point already moribund. To live at all is to pick out pertinent signals from the noise, organize one's own dynamics and actively plan paths to follow. As it turns out, even if the logic of our inventions should escape us, we are capable of modifying the ambient conditions that modify us, of reprogramming what programs us, by *mutual* adaptation. We have seen that each cultural niche, in the course of history, selects against a virtual whole of available innovations the technology pertinent to it, as a living organism "deducts" its useful information from the surrounding noise. As each nervous system of a life-form in the animal kingdom organizes its own world in the world, so each social organization should be able to organize its microsphere in the current mediasphere. Those fearful of a neodeterminism of a technological stripe perhaps do not take adequately into consideration the continuous feedback loop at work between technology that proposes and society that disposes (an "eco-biological" loop as Edgar Morin would say). In any case, that ethics should make technics a point of contention puts great stress on a culture. And were it not to do so, how else could our societies negotiate what forms humanity will take with our machines? For the most crucial question is no longer "what and which essence is the essence of man?" but the, every bit as philosophical, question that is posed by human techno-genesis: "What is really possible, and what sort of man can appear on the horizon tomorrow?" "Wherever there is danger," Hölderlin said, "there too grows what can save us." This futurology of the will cannot not include today a technology understood with Simondon as an "inductive and general science of the patterns of technical developments"—a science competent to indicate to us the most probable evolution of each line of descent of major mechanical systems. As much as misreading these evolutions can convert them into determinisms, progress in mediological knowledge can in the same measure increase our power of emancipation. Prediction, knowledge, and ability are here the primary goals. To *foresee* the directions and proclivities of systems still to emerge (since general tendencies are not unpredictable)—which includes the reduction of factors contributing to inertia, mobility, smaller and smaller equipment and microprocessors, further compression of data, more sophisticated graphics and so on—and to *know* what one wants (whether to live through the intermediary of screens, for example) are what is needed in order to *be able* to make do with or without or by opposing certain conditions, and on what terms. And this prudent distance would not merely be here the reluctant resignation of the concession that "we simply have to make do" (with the new technologies), but the active ambition to transform our culture into an organized offensive of memory. Not to do nothing more than administer these stores of traces given the name "patrimonies," but to re-inscribe the ancient legacies with bullish determination in new productions of the unknown. Is this not the challenge that a Diderot took up in an earlier day, in such high spirits, when he engaged head-on the arts and trades of his time?

It would be a loss at any rate for philosophy not to make its meanings where the future of human beings is played out, within *technè*, certainly even more than in the century of the Enlightenment. Facing the enigma of the present, may the researcher at least dare to adopt the poet's motto according to René Char: "My métier is state-of-the-art."

PART TWO

IN DEFENSE OF THE IMAGE

A Note about Context

This text was presented as part of the dissertation defense for the doctorate in philosophy at the Sorbonne (Paris I) on October 23, 1993, to a committee composed of François Dagognet (minutes), Alain Gras (chairman), François Guéry and Jacques Perriault.

Images, Not Signs

Author's Note

I will surprise no one here by admitting that *A History of the Western Eye*—as the title's cavalier capaciousness sufficiently demonstrates—was not written from the vantage point and under the constraints of a doctoral thesis.* I express particular thanks for your willingness to consider it such. But it would be misleading to deny that with all this dissertation's lacunae and hastinesses, there is behind it a set of theses or hypotheses relating less to the nature of the visual image than to the manner in which images are approached and written about. I will first offer some remarks about what this method of mediological analysis should not be confused with, what its proper object should be, what already established idea it opposes, toward which conclusions, finally, it leads. This will entail discussing possible misunderstandings, a conception taking realia and concrete problems for its subject, a sure contradiction and some possible implications. These issues aim to bridge past and future.

I. Disciplinary Neighbors and Creditors

A history of the West's collective cultures of the eye is not the same thing as a *phenomenology* of the visible like those that

---

* *Vie et mort de l'image: une histoire du regard en Occident* (Paris: Gallimard, 1992). The following text can be read as a methodological or theoretical introduction to this larger study of art and media. [Trs.]

Merleau-Ponty deployed so well (particularly in his "Eye and Mind"*). In other words, reconstructing the succession of regimes of vision is not to be confused with an inquiry into the pre-predicative origin of *seeing*. Such inquiries seek to get inside the texture of Being, to delineate the miracle of sensed sentience, the enigma of the human body and its experience of the world. There will be found here no search for a *latent* layer of meaning, otherwise beclouded, beneath a *manifest* layer of the visible. No illusion to denounce, no orthodoxy to dismantle—in short, nothing to demystify. Instead of the depth approach of the phenomenologist, we have preferred (modestly, I think) to analyze differentially the modalities of "seeing" by approaching the practices of visual figuration historically, in an entirely external way.

To go back upstream from the visible to what it was that historical communities of the eye actually "had in view" might, making due allowance for other more obvious differences, seem to resemble one of those projects of "archeology" that followed in the wake of Michel Foucault. Its method is indeed at once historical—locating certain thresholds of discontinuity within what would appear a continuum, namely sight itself or the act of looking [*le regard*]—and *descriptive*, that is, non-normative, concerned to exclude judgments of value as much as possible. But our approach has little in common with a history of Reason (or of madness, the shadow it casts). We have sought to go back to the regimens of belief [*régimes de croyance*] that lay behind not so much what Foucault called constituted bodies of knowledge or discursive formations but rather behind the art forms or artifacts we consider. Nor have we considered the oeuvre of a given set of painters or even a given genre or figural style as marking a pertinent and distinct artistic articulation. Our interests go farther back than those of an art history that vaunts the unity of works from a given period, carefully inspects what is internal to their organizational principles, jumps from one celebrated artist's name to the next. They are distant from those histories of Forms that have set up camp in that prideful and

*Maurice Merleau-Ponty, "Eye and Mind," tr. Michael B. Smith, in Galen A. Johnson and Michael B. Smith, eds, *The Merleau-Ponty Aesthetics Reader: Philosophy and Painting* (Evanston: Northwestern University Press, 1993), pp. 121–49. The essay was originally published as "L'Oeil et l'esprit" in *Art de France* (January 1961). [Trs.]

rather incestuous insularity named "art," in which images engender other images.

We want to reach back further too, we should add, than a social history of art in the distinguished lineage of the Warburg and Courtauld school (in which stand out for us the illustrious names of Gombrich, Baxandall, Alpers and Haskell). Certainly their type of history runs counter to that practiced by an Aloïs Riegl, or a Wölfflin, the so-called "internalists." It establishes a concrete correlation between societal and artistic causal series of representations—paintings seen as the result of a collaboration between painter and public. It has the merit of avoiding sociological reductionism by citing as historical evidence on a case by case basis the relevant *mediators*, the "way stations" between ideas and works as Baxandall would have it (investors of capital, owners, patrons, dealers, etc.)—or, in another classical formulation (Panofsky's), between Gothic architecture and medieval scholasticism. But our approach sets itself apart from these for two readily apparent reasons. The first, which is nevertheless more in keeping with the level of conceptual generality of the social-historical studies, has to do with our concern to derive some categorical taxonomy out of the flux of historical change. This is foreign to those inquiries in the Anglo-Saxon mold which take exception to totalizing theories for moving to a "global" reality by minutely examining the singularity of one object or case study, an "interconnecting network of microscopic relations" (Carlo Ginzburg). These English historians deliberately operate within a more restricted historical focus—on "Rembrandt's studio" or "the Quattrocento eye." Out of this concentrated range comes the strength of these studies, from which we have drawn and profited a great deal. But our second reason finds fault with the disadvantage of precisely this positive or positivist scholarly asset. Without a focal point taking in a greater historical breadth these authors do not critically examine the notions of which they make use: those of "art," "work," "taste," "art criticism," etc. A Francis Haskell for instance writes the history of the fluctuations and successive rediscoveries of Western taste (how Romanesque art was invented toward 1818, favorably reappraised not long after the wave of Gothic art, and so on) but not the history of the idea of taste, of what made its conception possible in the first place.

By contrast, remaining nominally for the moment within the purview of aesthetics (which we take to have been only a transitional phase), our study borders more directly on a sociology of artistic perception like that which has been undertaken by Pierre Bourdieu. Bourdieu jettisons quite willingly the analysis of essence, substituting for ontological questions the question of the genesis of aesthetic positionings. His work is far removed from the celebrative discourses and phenomenologies, all more or less ecstatic; far from them in its problematizing of concepts handed down from the tradition of the esthetes, and in its redirecting of "art" toward socially constructed habits and beliefs—toward the historical work that went into instituting an autonomous field of activity and consumption. Why not, then, acknowledge here the debt we owe him?

There are other paths by which our analysis of the conditioning of historical possibilities that produced the concept *oeuvre d'art* (witness the landscape or self-portrait) joins up with the conclusions of the sociologist. Yet I venture to say they do not stop only there. Our history of "visual efficacies" needs to be written in two columns: the one that takes account of the material equipment or "tool kit" enabling the fabrication, display and distribution of objects of sight, and the other which chronicles the belief systems in which they were inscribed. (For one can speak equally of the technology of vision and the credulity of vision.) The institution of looking "aesthetically" in the West (the second moment of the tripartite periodization of the history of its eye we propose) sends us back to its gradual divesting of the habits of looking "idolatrously" (the first moment) and with that, therefore, back to a cultural history of religious adhesions. Thus the critical demystification of our scholarly speculations on art needs to better understand its core subject by entering into the *theological field* (to which I will return below). It needs also, as part of the same movement, to transfer a certain amount of intellectual capital to the *technical field*. This is necessary not only because the successive attempts by movements of modern art to purify the plastic object of its traditional parameters of referentiality (such as Impressionism, Cubism, Futurism, *Art cinétique* [1920], etc.) can quite largely be explained by the external competition from black and white photography, film, montage, etc. with their original status as non-art forms. It is necessary also because the social production of the artist is dependent on the modalities for producing the art *object*—modalities which determine in turn how the art *market* is constructed. The notion of the work as a unique object in its liability to private appropriation, or more widely the crowning notion of originality as a criterion for what is "artistic," did not constitute merely ideological and commercial concepts but also *industrial* ones (indeed because in opposition to the "industrial"). "Technical reproducibility" involved modification of the conditions under which the heretofore original object was produced. As Michel Melot has notably demonstrated, from the time of the first print reproductions an important determining factor for the changing criteria of the art market was the artificial rarefication of multiple copies and of the social prestige it accorded potential acquirers (through limited runs of pieces of sculpture, numbered photographic prints, so-called engraved "artist's proofs" of lithographs, etc.). These were effects which redounded back onto the nature of the *objet d'art* itself.[1] To offer evidence that "the quality of the artwork is independent from the quality 'artwork'" (as Melot puts it) is to finally recognize the essential correlation between technics and aesthetics.

The sociologist tends to describe a world of *subjects without objects*; the technologist a world of *objects without subjects*. The originality of the mediological approach, as far as it may be granted, would consist *in multiplying the bridges that can be thrown up between the aesthetic and the technological*. (This takes it further than simply trying to reconcile substances and forms, or better still the material and mental devices that collaborate to mold belief and have led human beings to have faith in the characteristic shapings of their culture.) Such bridges are established in practice between subjects and objects which in each epoch construct one another. We must remind the sociologist, on the one hand, that there are real objects, that they have a history and that this material history is decisive; and the *student of technology*, on the other, that the decisive history of

[1] Michel Melot, "La Notion d'originalité et son importance dans la définition des objets d'art," *Sociologie de l'art*, Congrès de la Société française de sociologie, Marseilles, 1986. This account includes a perspicacious analysis of Duchamp's readymade as a "vaccination against the serialized object."

formal procedures and machines is not solitary, and that no technical innovation can take place without just as soon being
mediated by its milieu and social relations.

II. From Essence to Efficacy

To speak of the visual artifact we will be using that volatile and
protean French term *image* in its objectively material signification
as "picture" in English (excluding its natural, mental or literary
senses). We have not sought to ask the question of its "essence"
(What *is* an image?) nor of semantics (What is *meant* by images as
representations?). We ask instead the pragmatic questions: How is
the image made? What can one do with it? Of what use is it to me?
We have fully espoused "the logic of usage" (taking up Jacques
Perriault's expression). The practice of devotion, of old; the practice
of taste, following that; and of making one's way among the land-
marks of visual fields, today: such a succession welds the supposed
intrinsic properties of "the" image to the changing relation we
have maintained in dialogue with it over a considerable course of
history at once optical and social-psychological.

If mediology poses the question of symbolic efficacy, the mediological study of images asks about the conditions of "iconic
efficacy" (following Daniel Bougnoux). What effects of imposi-
tion, receptivity, and fixation or stupefaction has the image been
able to develop as a function of its particular technologies of manufacture and our cultural systems of perception? These effects
have appeared to our historical scansions of the symbolic power of
images that produced them to be those of either "presence," "art"
or "information" (useful terms pedagogically or as simple indica-
tors). "Symbolic" comes from the Greek *symballein*, "to put back
together," "reunite," or "bridge": such a function is to our eyes
synonymous with the mediative function. Answering the questions "From what to what is the image a go-between?"; "With
what does it put us in relation?"; "What is it positioned to transmit to us?" would be to arrive at the concrete determination of the
symbolic operation a given image reinforces or supports, and
beyond that the type of visual attention a culture brings to it.

*

The history of the image and of looking is therefore a theory of *effects* and not of values (of truth or of beauty). Its premises from the start were closer to those of an "iconocracy" (Mondzain's term) than an iconology (Panofsky's). It is thus not a very catholic study, from the Greek *kath'holon* ("on the whole," "in general," "as a whole," "universally," "according to the plenitude of its attributes"): from the very outset it forsook questions about the means of knowledge for those about the stakes of power. There is indeed a cognitive and pedagogical use for the idea of the image *of things* in their worldliness, and that is the venerable Platonic problematic of illusion, deception by the senses, the double, the simulacrum—renewed in our day by the idea of accurate modelling or commensurateness, and literally turned around 180 degrees by the revolutions in generating images for scientific purposes. And there is a second problematic, more affective and dynamic, which orients us not toward the world but toward God and human beings: namely that of sacrilege and seduction, of iconoclasm and the "war of images." It extends, if you will, from Saint John of Damascus* to debates about "cultural exceptionalism." Or from the Byzantine icon as a "strategy for military occupation of the mind" (according to Marie-José Mondzain's formulation) to the Hollywood film as a similar strategy for occupying the worldwide totality of mimetic mirrors.[2] These two roles crisscross in reality but their respective spheres of interest and influence can, I think, be distinguished. Let us adopt the working

---

*The theologian John of Damascus (c. 675–c. 749) was the last of the Eastern church fathers. Under the protection of the Moslem khalif Abdul Malek at Damascus, he wrote and published in defense of icons as part of holy worship, against the Byzantine emperor Leo III's order to destroy sacred images during the iconoclast controversy. John argued for the essential continuity between man as the image of God (who in order to be imitated had to exist in nature), Christ as the Son in the image of the Father, and the depiction of proper religious subjects (saints, Christ as human being). His elaboration of such distinctions as that between *veneration* of images as a sign of submission and *adoration* (*latreia*) of the prototype due only to God contributed to a tradition of iconophilia that eventually proved acceptable to both Western and Eastern Churches (following the Seventh Council of Nicaea, 787). See for example selections from the writings in Appendix no. 7 of Hans Belting, *Likeness and Presence: A History of the Image before the Era of Art*, tr. Edmund Jephcott (Chicago: University of Chicago Press, 1994), pp. 503–5. [Trs.]

[2] See Marie-José Mondzain, *Espace de l'image et territoire à gouverner*, I.N.A., September 1993.

assumption that representational images have their pure and their practical reason. When their value resides chiefly in their application to the knowable, we can speak of "logical icons" (to use Peirce's term) such as diagrams, maps, schematic tables, geographical plottings, etc.—icons that are visual but not figural. Figural images, assessed in their impact or influence on the senses, would include "analogical icons" which resemble what they represent—characteristic of paintings, frescoes, any photographically produced print, film frames, etc. We found at the beginning of our study that the mediological option, needing as it does to pay particular attention to how power is projected rather than how bodies of knowledge become elaborated, led us toward images as *intentionally directed* objective media or vehiculations, intermediary between man and man, inspected publically and displayed purposively—like exhibits in a criminal case. We were drawn less to the image *of* an object (versus *as* an object), intermediary between man and nature, whose role is to render the real "visible, readable and foreseeable" by means of the triptych "figuring, charting, and modeling." This is why the television screen (which serves the interests of directing or seducing viewers ideologically) answered far more to our preoccupations in this work than the computer screen (a means for discovery and intellection). In this way we have deliberately put aside the tradition of philosphical questions about the essence of images and imagery in favor of their existential conditioning. That is, in order to approach from a fresh angle the question of "essence" itself.

Only yesterday François Dagognet's *Philosophie de l'image* (1984) made the argument that visual images as a means of communication have "taken on a life of their own and broken free of their secular wrappings." He exorted us in short to "think about visual communication and the changes it has undergone historically." We have attempted to do just this, but rather by conceiving of the image *through* its changes. Once again, not in order to arrive at an essentialist "eidetic variation" or abstract invariant of "the" image, which could only be an elusive and non-existent essence. When Dagognet says *"and* the changes it has undergone," this hardly indicates a mere supplemental bit of information. We have sought to take seriously the material procedures of manufacturing, projecting and diffusing visual representations because it became apparent that a modification of productive technique brought with it a change in the very nature and status of the product. The ontology of images is answerable to such technique: one simply does not take the same kind of photograph using a photographic plate exposed for two hours during the subject's tedious pose and using a Polaroid camera. And as Dagognet frequently reminds us, for a century technical progress has brushed away from representational images all those obstacles which iconophobic denigration had for twenty-five centuries declared most philosophically objectionable and insurmountable: silver salt emulsions have given us color photography beyond the shadowy insubstantiality of black and white; film endowed images with movement; X-rays, tomography, scanning and M.R.I.'s have brought to light the interior of the body and its hidden structures; and digital remixing [*production numérique*] has dislodged the pre-eminence of the original over the copy to the point of reversing the order of the real and its re-staging, replacing anteriority by the criterion of actuality.

Walter Benjamin revised how we think about artistic creation by suggesting that the means of mechanical reproduction changed "the essence of art itself."* Cannot all categories of produced images be looked at in this way, from the underground cave paintings of the Neolithic to the synthesized imagery of virtual reality? The more recent history of the visual arts gives all the more cause for adopting such a perspective in their increasing need for engineered systems of support, their ever-growing technological dimensions—from those of the photographic camera to the computer. (If film is only *in one of its respects* an industry, television was so at its very inception.) No longer is the configuration of equipment a factor only in the latter stage of reproduction "downstream" following creation, as in Benjamin's time; it now figures prominently in the very conception of the work, "upstream" at the source. It is thus impossible, when confronting images, to bring philosophical rigor to their history

*Walter Benjamin, "The Work of Art in the Age of Mechanical Reproduction," in Harry Zohn, tr., *Illuminations*, ed. Hannah Arendt (New York: Schocken Books, 1969). [Trs.]

without first listening to or reading students of technology. For us this has meant not relegating to the side-aisles of "material history" or to the lower ranks of a "semiology of visual messages" numerous developments of visual culture: the evolution of materials and craftsmanship of painting by hand (tempera, encaustic, oil, acrylic); the archaic machines of the baroque marvelous (windmills and pumps, fountains, cranes and *grottes animées*); the procession of the first projecting machines of vision (magic lanterns, fantascopes, panoramas, praxinoscopes, etc.); and the crucial early babblings of pre-cinema from the crankable chronophotographic invention of Marey on.

All this means, again, not setting off to study the "utterance" or the "iconic narrative," the "imagistic signifier" or "the representational image as 'sign,'" as some bright intelligences for whom all is linguistic (or rather, for whom language can be reduced only to its signs) have done. One must *first* ask what species of image one is dealing with, on what material support system or perspectival apparatus they rely, in what setting they are seen, and with what device they have been reproduced. The image when formed on a screen by the projection of light behind a photographic frame of film across a darkened room belongs to a different order of "signs" from the image electronically induced by a cathodic current on a luminiferous surface. One does not comprehend in the same categories the *object-image* of film, the *effect-image* of television (effected by sequential scanning), and the *project-image* of virtual reality (a prolongation of the body in a "clone" or construct or model of anticipation). In each instance the viewer changes to a different space: the plastic and solid space of film, the diffused and ductile space of television, the interactive and encompassing universe of "cyberspace." And to a different time: the deferred time of a plotted dramatic representation (that is, film, which is also *recorded* on acetate rather than instantly transmitted by cameras), the immediacy of live broadcast (brought to you directly from the scene by television), and the constructed time of televirtuality. When one is said to be *facing* the movie screen, transported *behind* the TV screen or tube, and *inside* a virtual environment we are speaking not about changing points of view but about a change in the very nature of visibilia from medium to medium. We know of no coherent

"system of the image" which underlies the genres of icon, painting, photography, novelized illustrations (*photo-roman*), comic
strip, cinema, television, etc. We have encountered only systems
that organize variously the act of looking. To state these findings
in another way: if it is true that the linguist has been able to form
the idea of "language" starting from the natural languages and
justify it theoretically, I am not sure one can repeat the same
process of abstraction out of images sculptured versus pictorial
versus photographic versus audiovisual, etc. An *iconistics* as a
general science of images to place beside linguistics would seem
to be an illusory objective.

From semiology's object to our own we see the inversion of content and form: what the former calls the "pragmatic context" of
an interpretation of a given visual representation we have sought
to make our text, our corpus of study. And what before has passed
for the "signification" of the visual phenomenon is for us simply
semantic context. Among other things such context can turn out to
be the physical situation of the viewer determining the psychological effects of the viewed object or image. The context of cinematic
viewing produces a reality effect [*effet du réel*] unlike that of television viewing. Wrapped in the movie house's darkened anonymity
that Roland Barthes characterized as "pre-hypnotic," I am riveted
to the screen's reflections. They swallow me up. You cannot tear
yourself away; the deception could hardly be more alluring, the
promise of ecstasy fuller. Even the body's own motive forces have
been blocked. I can of course turn my head away or close my eyes,
yet such gestures of refusal here are unnatural. This is so not only
because I have paid to watch and am seated in a row amidst
strangers, but because the projected sequences' continuity will not
sag, immersing me *ne varietur* in compelling successions of images
independent of my will. The TV screen by contrast is not watched
within an institutional setting devised for spectators. One is not
physically immobilized, activity is not totally suspended, viewers
can still speak out or to one another. There is no discontinuity of
everyday space and time because one remains at home, *en famille*,
within a hyperfamiliar commodity. A movie-watcher *attends* a
public screening as if it were a ceremony or staged spectacle, but
not a privatized broadcast directed toward you and your domicile.
From this latter arises a floating televisual attention, frothy and

drawn to tid-bits, which results in the paradox that to TV's height-ened effect of reality corresponds a state of lowered vigilance. The film experience styles itself as a distraction that stands out against my daily routine of time and local space, while television contin-ues to inform us, without breaks or remove from the daily world. This is precisely what induces a stronger suggestibility in TV "viewers" who don't really view (in a contemplative sense) at all. The filmic dream is dreamed nocturnally, while TV reverie takes place like a day-dream, a semi-activity in a state of distracted wakefulness. No doubt the dreamer cannot know that he is dreaming whereas the audience of a film knows they are at the the-ater (a dream cut up into scheduled showings and intermissions with people forming lines outside would be tawdry indeed). So film would be more akin to a *deliberate dream*, a voluntary but extreme somnambulism, and the television broadcast rather more an offering of the real, in its *juste milieu*, yet captured in twilight tones and half-tints.

Against the idealizing approach taken by classical philosophy (including Sartre) we have thus not hesitated to treat the "image" as a concretely produced object [*"chosifier" l'image*] that it might be better understood and recovered. It proved necessary to confront fully the materiality of visual representation—its *sur-faces* (walls, parchments, wood, canvas), its constituent *elements* (pigments, precious metals), its *machinery*. For doctrines of poet-ics copy from and follow technologies—which always catch up short our extant habits of perception and the prevailing socially received hierarchies among the arts. Think for example about all that a miniscule technical innovation like the remote control button is in the process of changing in the way we look at things and in our culture at large, promoting *discontinuousness, juxta-position*, and the cult of the most intense temporal sequence that can grab one's attention. Here too we find still another variation on circulating not within but among images.[3] The shopper for the little screen's wares gets used to taking up a narrative at any

---

[3] On this score see the analyses that have been made by Jean-François Barbier Bouvet (Director of the Bayard Press series), notably *Lire la page comme une image* (avail-able in manuscript, 1993). [In the American context one might make the case for the influence of "channel-surfing" or "-grazing" or of the format and color graphics of a paper like *USA Today* (which has been called "McPaper"). Trs.]

one of its points of entry. The replacement of syntactical subordination by parataxis is something to be investigated in visual sequences as much as for written ones: it is nothing less than another mode of reading and composing. And of producing the prototype paste-up of the first page of a newspaper.

III. The Image is Not a Language

Focusing on the mutations of technology made us from the outset adversaries of the glories of semiology. The project of "making a discourse that would hold to the image and be one *of* images rather than *about* them," in the late Louis Marin's formulation, was not our own. As far as we are concerned a "symbolic" function is not *ipso facto* "semiotic." To mix the regimens of seeing and saying under the general notion of the sign, without distinguishing further the different *genres* of sign, would have led to an impasse. An image component of course finds its way daily into texts, and the textual appears in and beneath visual forms—from titled engravings to today's (scripted) audiovisual imagery. Let us be clear that such "symbiotic" objects of looking, such "icono-texts" (novels "told" photographically or calligrams) do not derive their effect, when seen, from the *confusion* of elements; quite the contrary, their heterogeneity lends value to the mixture.*
An "iconology" that would take credit for having folded the visible back into the readable would indeed risk trading the illegitimacy of its postulates on the sterility of its results. The order of language is not generalizable to all disorders of sense and meaning, and it behooves us without regret to be resigned to the experiences of looking as an irremediable, or shall we say inestimable, disorder with its own logic.

What has passed for self-evidence here has to do not only with a beautiful mirage of academics, but with that daily regimen of metaphors to which we cleave when we speak of "reading paintings," the "language of film," the "grammar of styles," "pictorial

---

*Think for example of the filmed version of a novel. Surely what was before written at great length must be further compressed as dialogue and plot, visual characterization and *mise en scène* ("the page becomes stage"). But does this mean it is any less enhanced by the collaboration and quality of *both* its writerly and screened virtues? [Trs.]

vocabulary," "figurative grammar" and so on. Let it be said here that this amounts to a misuse of language which in the very hey-day of the *superstition linguistique* in the early sixties Dina Dreyfus (who initiated the first series of televised philosophy courses in French) did her utmost to dispel.[4] While the sign as a (minimally) perceptible materiality gives way to its meaning, she argued, "a visual image can never be overlooked as a perceived object except under penalty of disappearing pure and simple." She and others proposed that we concede painting's status as an object that *has signification yet does not strictly signify*, as it cannot be decomposed into discrete unities coming under a "doubly articulated system" (the linguistic axes of paradigm and syntagm). One can "decipher" such an object like a cryptogram but not "decode" it. The difference is that a decoding can claim it is exhaustive, while a deciphering can only uncover layers of superposed meanings regarding an always undecidable and ambiguous object. A road sign is univocal, a closed signal; there is every reason to speak of the "code of the road." But the image that one calls a product of art is polysemous and ambiguous. One might think of it as a visual ideogram enclosed within the determination of the conventional sign, always the promise of another thing, an infinite equivocation, a knot of possibilities. To have a "code" it will not suffice that there be two opposed levels or planes creating an uncertain intelligibility; there still is needed a set rule of correspondence between those levels. The archaic pagan idol or the Chistian icon is, if you will, a two-sided sign, visible and invisible, natural and supernatural. A certain Greek statue is at the same time Athena in person, her immediate living presence, and an object of gold and ivory placed in a temple of the Acropolis. In a restricted sense one can say that its "referent" is divinity, and that this tangible thing makes a "sign" or gesture directed toward a sacred presence. But not that this presence is its "signified"—nor that this particular statue obeys a syntax. Were this true there would then be cases of unacceptable statuary figures contravening the combinatory rule postulated by the syntactical system in question. Yet no correspondence is forbidden: as Jean-Pierre Vernant tells us, in the Greek world any shaped form can "stand for any

---

[4] See the *Revue de l'enseignement philosophique*, nos 3/4, February–May 1962.

divinity." Whereas a grammar can only be a set of rules determining incompatibles.*

Will not the science of signs have sufficiently progressed to invalidate the intellectual effort Carolingian Church doctors deemed
indispensable, when in the ninth century they drew a distinction
between the abstraction of the *signum* and imitative representation
provided by the *imago* or the *figura*? At that time they set up an
opposition between the *signum crucis* or the Constantinian cross,
drawn or made as a gesture with the hands, and the *imago crucifixi*,
the three-dimensional crucifix in wood or carved ivory.[5] Certainly
ornamental art suggests an intermediate level between the two poles,
but it should take nothing away, evidently, from the primary

---

*Debray's clear demarcation of the text/image boundary parallels others that have been
made within the Anglo-American tradition of aesthetic theory and analytical philosophy
of symbolic systems. Though they are seldom as purist in disqualifying the vocabulary of
some process of semiotics or notation in speaking about pictorial and verbal signs, they
invariably return to textual communication as based on a system of differentiation (following Saussure) and pictures as inherently composite or synthetic or semantically
"dense." Following Nelson Goodman, W.J.T. Mitchell has discussed the question in
terms of "differentiation" versus "density," using Goodman's illustration of the graduated
versus ungraduated thermometer. "With a graduated thermometer," writes Mitchell,

> every position of the mercury is given a determinate reading: either the mercury has reached a cer-
> tain point on the scale or it is read as being closest to that point. A position between any two
> points on the scale does not count as a character in the system; we round off to the closest deter-
> minate reading. In an ungraduated thermometer, on the other hand, no unique, determinate
> reading is possible at *any* point on the thermometer: everything is relational and approximate,
> and every point on the ungraduated scale (an infinite number, obviously), counts as a character
> in the system. Every tiny difference in the level of the mercury counts as a different indication of
> the temperature, but none of the differences can be assigned a unique, determinate reading. There
> is no possibility of finite differentiation or the 'articulation' of a single reading . . . A picture is
> normally 'read' in something like the way we read an ungraduated thermometer. Every mark,
> every modification, every curve or swelling of a line, every modification of texture or color is
> loaded with semantic potential. Indeed, a picture, when compared to an ungraduated ther-
> mometer or a graph, might be called a 'super-dense' or what Goodman calls a 'replete' symbol,
> in that relatively more properties of the symbol are taken into account. . . . The image is syn-
> tactically and semantically dense in that no mark may be isolated as a unique, distinctive
> character (like a letter of an alphabet), nor can it be assigned a unique reference or 'compliant.'
> Its meaning depends rather on its relations with all the other marks in a dense continuous field.

W.J.T. Mitchell, *Iconology: Image, Text, Ideology* (Chicago: University of Chicago
Press, 1986), p. 67. On Debray's terms one might fault the use of the term "syntacti-
cally" in this account because though one may judge a representational object of
variable quality in what it attempts to portray, it cannot be binarily-summarily dismissed
as "ungrammatical." [Trs.]

[5] See Jean-Claude Schmitt, *La Voie occidentale des images*, I.N.A., 15 September 1993.

distinction between the two orders of material and conceptual reality to which attests the most current thinking on the matter.

Needless to say, what is most flagrantly particular to the messages of visual forms did not escape the semiologists' sagacity. We recall first their observation that the speaking subject plays no role in either the making or the immediate perception of images. Painting is mute poetry, said Poussin, following Horace and Simonides.* After that we are reminded of the primacy of the spatial over the temporal. A painting, an engraving, a photograph evade the linear succession of language through the co-presence of their parts. They are apprehended *en bloc* by the intuition, in an instantaneous perceptive synthesis—the *totum simul* of vision. A visual image arrests the flow of time like a syncope,† contracts the string of moments.

---

*Rhetorical criticism (not to mention poetry) has of course made much scholastic hay out of the *ut pictura poesis* conceit. Among the two most frequently cited studies are probably Jean H. Hagstrum, *The Sister Arts: The Tradition of Literary Pictorialism from Dryden to Gray* (Chicago: University of Chicago Press, 1958) and Murray Krieger, *Ekphrasis: The Illusion of the Natural Sign* (Baltimore: The Johns Hopkins University Press, 1992). Ekphrasis, as not only verbal description but the conceit that the art object itself "speaks," is the other side of the coin inscribing painting as mute poetry. For a study that follows this motif against the background of politics and the post-Revolutionary museum in select poems, criticism and novels of English and French writings in the nineteenth century, see Eric Rauth, *The Work of Memory: Ekphrasis, Museums, Memorialism in Keats, Quatremère de Quincy, Balzac and Flaubert* (Princeton University diss., 1990).

More recent art theory, however, has seen fit to deconstruct the *ut pictura poesis* simile, eroding the experiential borders between the silence of the visual arts and the verbality of discourse. It asserts that painting is in fact "discursive," especially insofar as its subjects can be "read" and have historically taken part in the circulation of discourse in society. For a synoptic discussion of the premises of this approach see the introduction by Norman Bryson, ed., *Calligram: Essays in New Art History from France* (Cambridge: Cambridge University Press, 1988), pp. xiii–xxv. Many representative essays, influenced by the semiotics Debray takes to task, can also be found in Norman Bryson, Michael Ann Holly, and Keith Moxey, eds, *Visual Theory: Painting and Interpretation* (New York: HarperCollins, 1991). [Trs.]

†Debray's term *syncope* matches the word in English. Both are derived from the Greek *synkopē*, a cutting up, and *synkoptein*, to break, and have a medical as well as grammatical usage. In physiology syncope is a swoon or unconsciousness due to cerebral anemia from a slowing or stopping of heartbeats accompanied by lowered respiration. (It is quite similar to what Paul Virilio has "diagnosed" as *picnolepsy* [see his *The Aesthetics of Disappearance*, tr. Philip Beitchman (New York: Semiotext(e), 1991)].) In grammar it refers to eliding one or more letters from within a word, as "ne'er" for "never," "Gloster" for "Gloucester," or the French "*dénoûment*" for "*dénouement*." [Trs.]

And at the origin of every contemplative deliberation or lingering, every meticulous searching look or scrutiny, every progressive appropriation of figural space, flashes that lightning or sudden stabbing pain, the shock into awareness of a first contact (*le plaisir visuel*, like other pleasures, resembles a halt of time's passage).

Of course the semiologist will see no difficulty here because "the conceptual apparatus of semiology is more general than that of linguistics" (in Umberto Eco's words). The semiotic universe, ranging from the communicative signals read by animals to "kinesics" or body language semiology, stretches beyond language and precedes it. It will be made clear to us that every code does not have to be a language, just as every message does not have to be speech. Verbal signs are but an individual case of *ségnicité* or semiosis (Eco again). From an analysis of language, semiology drew its idea of the code, a formal network of logical relations; then, finding it indispensable to project widely the operations of decoding well beyond its original field of validity, it put forth that language was a particular form of code and that the absence of code did not automatically follow from the absence of language per se. It was a genial if not demonstrable inference, which helped answer the objections that it unduly extrapolated from linguistic rules to extra-linguistic domains. It especially helped to set an object as obviously non-linguistic as representational images among "discursive phenomena," giving them the status of signifying objects.

The ordinary image or picture has much in common, in Peirce's terminology, with the "icon" or analogical sign, characterized by a relation of natural resemblance with its referent, missing as such the arbitrariness defining the "symbol" or linguistic sign. The difficulties are apparent when one tries to segment the chromatic or linear continuum of a painting or film shot, even more so a sculpture's volume—of any plastic object in three dimensions—into distinctive unities of the morpheme and phoneme type, whose value depends on their positional relation of *opposition* to the other units (like the tones and notes of a musical piece). In response to this (not without attempting to divide as well a formal image into pertinent portions) the semiologician will say that "resemblance itself is codified," that "the 'natural' imitation by the iconic sign of the object to which it refers" is of the socio-cultural type founded on the "conventionality of codes of imitation" (Eco). The worlds of analogy can thus be brought into the fold of semiotic interpretation though marginalized and *in extremis*. An obliging elasticity of notions will, then, allow one to speak of "uncertain paradigmatics" (Metz), "weak encoding" (Eco) with a basis in the "more or less" (rather than the yes or no). Metalanguages can then be invented, subsuming given paradigms as "virtual" syntagms or grammars, ascending the ladder of complications. The motion picture offered a tempting corpus because of its technical basis in *découpage* and intercalations of separate units—frames of film. Its chronological procession, or filmic narrativity, provided the equivalent to verbal syntagms in the form of sequences, which were held to function in turn as paradigms (thematically, "metaphorically," etc.) in relation to the film-syntagm. It seemed as if the comic strip presented more grist preordained for the semiological mill, with its framed vignettes which a "stripology" can analyze into lexical units shaping their reading, even more structurally intelligible than the evanescent cinematic object because so easily and fixedly reproduced.

But the optimal material for any "rhetoric of the image" was the illustrated advertisement, aptly identified by Roland Barthes in his well-known article as a "virtual piece of cake" [*facilité considérable*], a pretty straightfoward specimen: the product was the referent; its attributes, the signifieds; the sponsoring company, the sender; the consumer, the receiver.* Discriminating between literal and symbolic "messages" will quite naturally set the object itself, a "denotative signifier," against the "connotative signifieds" brought to attention by the given advertisement or commercial. (In common parlance, what is shown and what is evoked.) Here the second degree of communication is already collapsed into the first; semiotics' bestowal of an interpretive legitimacy on looking at the non-verbal part of commercial "art"—"art" which only promoted and never delivered the goods—could not have been better calculated to the advantage of

---

*Barthes' essay, "Rhétorique de l'image" originally appeared in *Communications* 4 (1964), pp. 40–51. A study in the Anglo-American context which parallels many of the concerns of Barthes' essay and *oeuvre* (though perhaps less "post-ideological" in its polemics) would be John Berger's *Ways of Seeing* (London: Penguin, 1973, 1977). [Trs.]

those parties who stood to benefit by the nominal advance in analytic power. For its practitioners, semiotics afforded intellectual respectability; for the audience it found, modernity was made solvent or creditworthy. This social contract has proven hard to resist. But is it scientifically sound and fertile?

The advertising message is for visual semiological coding and decoding a primary school lesson whose answers are written on the blackboard. A classical painting of mythological or biblical subject matter would correspond to the college entrance exams. A Ph.D. committee question might be photojournalism—wonderfully accidental, lacking all textual reference, the fragment of a world prior to its methodical cogitation and meaning, the thingliness of its depiction surpassing all discourse. Truly no one has answered it adequately without changing disciplines (transforming it into an examination question in literature or philosophy).

The debauchery of intelligence and virtuosity of semiology's interpretive acrobatics can be staggering. Their "readings" of images are tailor-made for wit and irony, but their results leave a perplexity. It is as if their authors find by the end of their analyses merely what they had initially put into them. It is not enough to keep steadfastly non-normative and borrow interpretive grids or templates from the most authoritative sources to acquire scientific rigor and positivity (the "mediology" I am proposing does not make such claims). This might perhaps be the lesson to draw from them.

Why have we spent so much time returning to these theorizings which have mostly miscarried by this day anyway? Because the dead languages that once spun so giddily around such airiness as "iconic utterance" underscore through contrast what is vital and rebellious in vision. Did not our poets have a better grasp of it than the theoreticians? Evoking marvels that "boast no witness but the wild eye," André Breton began *Surrealism and Painting*,

> The eye exists in its savage state . . . . It presides over the conventional exchange of signals that the navigation of the mind would seem to demand. But who is to draw up the scale of vision? . . . *

---

*André Breton, *Surrealism and Painting* [1928], tr. Simon Watson Taylor (New York: Harper and Row, 1972), p. 1. [Trs.]

To encode is to socialize (a language and a group go together). Such a gesture involves furthermore a will to curb the unsociable, to regularize what is irregular and disordered. Have we semiotized visual forms in order to be rid of them, dissolve their insistent barbarity in the analytical acid of linguistics? Do we stifle a scandalous and native ingenuousness proper to figuration, its unsettling "idiocy" ("idiotic" or *idios* in Greek being the private or particular as against the public man—the unschooled or ignorant)? Imitative images are idiotic because incapable of denoting the universal, cut off from generality and refractory toward all typification (one speaks far more often of "general ideas" than "general images"). They keep their silence from birth, being *in-fans* [Latin *in-*"not" + *fari-*"to speak"], irremediably enigmatic (words exist for every one; an image more for me, resembling me and in my measure). Language, semantics and syntax muzzle imagery, as if there has always been a fear of seeing or of the desire to see.* The feared dizziness of vision may be precisely its monstrous and intimidating silence. When Jean-Luc Godard one day responded to Canal Plus, which had asked him to produce a scripted text from which to work before filming *Histories of Film and Television*, he commented,

---

*For some readers in English, Debray's account of the antipathy to vision as an independent territory of experience—neglected by semiology and the post-war *sciences humaines* it influenced—may carry more conviction when situated in greater detail not only against the background of French structuralism and post-structuralism but also against the influence these movements have had in the Anglo-American academic context. For both, textuality and theories of representation have consistently been given more priority than the mimetic arts on their own terms. This may be due, in part, to the internal dialectics of a later Anglo-American criticism that rejected the New Critics' conceit of the "verbal icon," and a continental post-modernism that had little use for the sensory repleteness of phenomenology and *critique de la conscience*. On some of the reasons and historical precedents for this "denigration of vision in twentieth-century French thought" see Martin Jay's exhaustive *Downcast Eyes* (Berkeley: University of California Press, 1993). One could argue that post-modern critical preoccupations have replaced "looking" with "speculation," tableau with text. Debray proposes a historical investigation of the concrete and silent "ocular credulities" that, with some exceptions (Lévi-Strauss, the Annales School, etc.), have been less subject to study and verbalization as part of technologically and socially conditioned practices. [Trs.]

How strange that to confirm the necessity for such a project, one should ask for words on paper, when what I am really called on to do is tell, with images and sounds, the story of these images and sounds—the story of their marriage into a sonorous film print. Strange. As if the shadow of the written sentence were required as protection against the naive enlightening that comes from the screen. As if one had to "screen" (out) yet a second time, quote films merely as my transcribed memories, removing from them that prodigiously direct *force of presence* that had made of them the foremost and the only truly popular art form.

The man of words may perhaps feel vaguely inculpated when faced with "signs" without a code, with transmitting wordlessly. Perhaps one can interpret the semiological vogue and all its verbalizations of non-verbality as a return to the sender, a ruse to direct suspicion toward those irrationalists who evade the order of the code. We have witnessed learned efforts to return the crazy person in our attic to the reasonableness of speech, to conventionalize the natural, grammaticalize the sensorium, be clever, in a word. Might there not be behind them simply the refusal to accept a deep-set imagistic non-intelligibility which resists the Logos? Thus appears the symptom of hatred, the immemorial conjuration of the raw, the rough and the unrefined. To want anything natural to be a pseudo-nature, suspect any innocence, return the ill-gotten gains of "the illusion of the natural"—this was perhaps the *grande illusion* of the latest period of the human sciences. Beyond the revenge of the literate can be found a classic denial of animality, that is, of the natural.

The image as corporeality takes us back and short-circuits our humanities, interrupts courtesies, approaches making perceptible for us the idea of animality. It disrupts the smooth symbolic order of surfaces—like the flesh before and behind the Word. This eruption is more traumatizing still with what Peirce called the indexical fragment than with the icon: the index, a physical trace, may be recognized in that even animals are sensitized to it. Is not a photograph as affecting as an odor, unexpected and poignant? We might even think of it as an odor for the eye, set down and made perenially fresh by the material mount and chemical elements that received the graphic image of

a person long since fled; an odor that remains. Or a tiny fragment of portable, storable pelt. Of the images of which our
memories keep a remnant, can we not say they have gotten under
our skin? Looking should not only be taken as a placement at a
specular distance, it can become a contact, a caress or a palpation. The indexical fragment is at bottom unsayable and
unintentional: two discourtesies that do violence to civility (to the
world of works and acts of representation), and that in themselves are pure symbolic violations—committed against
symbolization itself by the eruption of the colorful and concrete.
An indexical "sign" of this sort (like the stenciled-in hand on the
cave walls at Lascaux), much like the analogical icon (of the
impressionist landscape type), awakens in the adult viewer fully
possessed of speech that "treasure of sighs, caresses and cries,"
that tumult of the *infans*, from before our appenticeships and
after our birth. There may well be a "rhetoric of the image," in
a manner of speaking, but so too in every image there is a
rhetoric transgressed.

It is always harder to explain the simple than the complex, the
originary than the late-in-the-day, the uncodable than the coded.
The precipitate reduction of the more complicated to the simpler
is labeled "reductionism." One could call the reverse movement
"Alexandrism": explaining the simple by the more complicated,
the labor at which semiological sophistication plugs away.
Despite all the exertion these logicians' logistics imply, they could
well be following our line of least resistance (the one we professional talkers go glibly down all the time). For a change, we
would like to go back *up* this discursive slope, extracting from
the conventional analysis' forward progress a confession that
one might have a right to regress backward, outside the field,
after all.

The barbarity or "idiotic" particularity of depicting versus
signing needed to be mentioned since that is exactly what
accounts for its superiority as an object of "mediological" study.
A figural form is better placed, and more suited, to pass into the
actuality of the act than is a discourse. The figural "surplus
value" resides in the image's deficit of code. It is its pre-semantic
dumbness (muteness) which confers on visual representation
exceptional powers that have so meagerly devolved to the text:

accessibility, credibility, affectivity, motivity, in proportions that defy any competition. Analogy is not impoverished meaning, as Barthes feared. It is magnanimous meaning.

At the surface of life, through an organized political expansionism or an innate penchant for vagabondage, an ensemble of images fills space, all spaces, dilates and circulates, freed from conventionalized use or function as language ordinarily is not, volatile and irrefutable because slipping through the social and territorial delimitations of linguistic competencies. It is a kind of Esperanto without combinatory rules for deriving vocabulary from known languages, a kind of superior market for all signs. (Nadar remarked of "Kodak" that it was "a word from Volapük, the language of the future, it seems.") I cannot read all forms of writing, but I can certainly, more or less well and without translator or dictionary, look at all images. I cannot learn Chinese without in some measure learning the history of China, but I can see a Chinese film and have its taste without knowing anything of the country's past. Between language which signifies without representing and the visual image where all signification is wrapped in a representational value, the competition is not even. Nor is the type of hold or influence they exert on us the same. When I arrive in Provence by car, passing by the Mont Sainte-Victoire visible from the highway, there is a sign telling me, "THE COUNTRYSIDE OF CÉZANNE"—and we all instantly understand, the Briton and Dutch person included. But a little further along the *autoroute*, beholding the landscape immortalized by Marcel Pagnol's books, I am informed by another roadsign that this is "THE *MASSIF* OF GARLABAN." Without Pagnol's novel *The Glory of my Father*, the sign would not however have been placed there, but those who are not French and pass by in their campers are probably not familiar with Pagnol. Here is the moral of the story which all empires have known, from the Byzantine to the American: if you want to make yourself known everywhere and establish dominion over the world, manufacture images instead of writing books. Of course postcards (=photograph + a bit of text on what it depicts) are not forbidden either; nor making films "based on the novel." But if everyone knows the name of their actors and directors, who cares about the screenwriters?

In terms of the depth of its psychological impact and staying power, the image sinks in and becomes anchored. The variations of memory were recently calculated in a poll using a scale of one hundred where advertisements which were primarily pictorial scored 117 and those primarily textual earned a 76. It is the emotive weight and assent or adherence compelled by visual messages which account for their irresistibleness. The Christians knew it fifteen centuries before the publicity agents: no proper catechism without sensory images. The concept will suffice to learn a doctrine, not for meeting a Person, and still less to be revivified and vitally transformed. Words speak to the intellect, but pious figural representations touch a consciousness attuned to embodied things. Whether one describes it as ravishment, pleasure or poignancy, under the heading of euphoria or anguish, the suspension of words is a sensual agitation which holds true in the case of mobilizing people and participation, physically. E-motion means "a putting into movement," *e*-"out" + *movere*-"to move." The didactic and mneumonic functions of the *Biblia idol-atarum*, advanced by Gregory the Great (c.540-604; pope from 590-604) in his famous letter from Marseilles, opened up a direct way to evangelization and the pastoral mission. The *punctum* dear to Barthes developed into the missionary *motus*, which is important in the *Evangelicae historiae imagines* (1593) of Nadal, "of great usefulness to the [Jesuit] company in the two Indies," recently studied by the exhibit on Sacred Images and Colonialism (the Banania infantryman and the "mysterious man of the desert"). It was the Jesuits, soldiers of God, who wittingly enlisted the iconography of the places and personnages of Christian theater, which allowed the faithful not only to better know the Savior, but to better love and thus to *follow him*. A pragmatics of the image historically must pass first through an erotics of the image.

Let us say in summation that the wish to extend discursive logics to cover the empire of visible forms is to miss at once the latter's two fundamental dimensions, strategic and libidinal; or to ignore the two potentialities that are at stake, political and amorous, the one because of the other.

IV. A Religious Materialism

It will not do, it seems, to consign all of these questions to a certain philosophical tradition, even if its logocentrism has been challenged. Plato notes in *Cratylus* (430 C) that there are two manners of representing a man: by a figural shape or by words. You either say his name or show his portrait.* Deciding which to use is not a dilemma of course; but in terms of values or valences, we find here, on the threshold of philosophical history, the matrix of a duality—a dichotomy both mythical and polemical (almost all theoreticians of visible forms like Plato show signs of a polemical relation to them). One could find its continuation through a sort of psychoanalysis of the qualities of the sensory world like that of Bachelard's.† There exists a tradition or rather a complex of iconophobia—at once a structure of thought and of sensibility—which links Plato to Sartre subterraneously. Without wanting to borrow from the classificatory passions of by-gone days their scholastic mania for dividing for its own sake, we submit a provisional table of respective iconophilic and iconoclastic values along these lines:

* " . . . Both sorts of imitation—I mean both pictures or words—are . . . equally attributable and applicable to the things of which they are the imitation" (Socrates). See the B. Jowett translation (3rd ed., 1892) in *The Collected Dialogues of Plato*, Edith Hamilton and Huntington Cairns, eds (Princeton: Princeton University Press, 1961), p. 464. [Trs.]

†Though most of Gaston Bachelard's work is concerned with the importance of rationality, concepts, and normativity in the history of science, an interest shared with Canguilhem and the Anglo-American history of science of Kuhn, Feyerabend, and others, he turned to an appreciation of the nonscientific or "poetic" imagery of human experience which can be shown historically to have acted as epistemological obstacles to a proper understanding of physical process—as Lamarck was misled by observing the sequence of color changes undergone by burning white paper to understand "combustion as a process whereby the 'violence' of the fire 'unmasks' the fundamental, underlying color of the paper (black) by stripping away successive chromatic layers" (Gary Gutting, *Michel Foucault's Archeology of Scientific Reason* [Cambridge: Cambridge University Press, 1989], p. 15). The example of Bachelard's shift in this part of his work from an interest in the history of epistemology to a "poetics" of imagery (as in *The Pyschoanalysis of Fire*, tr. A.C.M. Ross [Boston: Beacon Press, 1964]) would reinforce Debray's project of reconstructing the irrational, non-semiological history of visual forms as the medium of collective psychologies of religious and political belief. [Trs.]

IMAGE	LANGUAGE
NATURE (*Phusis*)	CULTURE (*Nomos*)
PASSIVE PRINCIPLE: matrix matter as receptacle (concave)	ACTIVE PRINCIPLE: seed informing form (convex)
BODY	SPIRIT
FEMININE (sensuality, latidudinarianism)	MASCULINE (austerity, puritanism)
MIMETICISM (trickery)	SYMBOLISM (certitude)
PLEASURE PRINCIPLE (seduction)	REALITY PRINCIPLE (correction)
VALUES OF THE PERCEPTIBLE: art, instinct, intuition	VALUES OF THE INTELLIGIBLE: knowledge, distance, deduction
ANTI-VALUES OF THE HOT: pollution, impurity, disease	ANTI-VALUES OF THE COLD: violence, repression, aridity
COPY (assures reproduction)	ORIGINAL (assures procreation)
MEDIATING ENTITY (the "by means of") The Holy Virgin, or the setting	MEDIATED ENTITY (the "what") The Word, or the scenario
THREE-DIMENSIONAL (popular, accessible)	TWO-DIMENSIONAL (elitist, steep road)
SPACE ("Space is a Woman")	TIME ("Time is a Man"—Blake)
THE CONTINUOUS	THE DISCONTINUOUS
POLYTHEISM (sin)	MONOTHEISM (salvation)

It bears repeating: a table as naive as this need not mean that one must choose between visible and verbal, play one against the other as if each were an air-tight world sealed upon itself. Christian Metz stated correctly that "The analogous and the encoded cannot be set against one another in a clear opposition." Their combinations, over-determinations and cross-referencing cannot be discounted, since all the indications are that hybrid entities prove the most interesting (pictures with legends, drawings with captions, talking films, etc.). So it is far from our intention to entertain answering the imperialism of the sign with an irredentism of the picture. But it is not an unreasonable exaltation of imagery into a stronghold to want to bring to light (were it only by making an inventory of persistent fantasies) what is proper to figuration in the face of the discursive. (This with the understanding that neither one has an existence and a meaning except in relation to the other.)

I have had to coin a perilous oxymoron to condense the method underlying the span of centuries traversed by my history of looking—"religious materialism." The paradox was intended as a safeguard to ensure that the methodological equipment would not make us disregard what was essential: the declensions of that "perceptual faith" Merleau-Ponty had so helpfully uncovered a while back, but which he persisted (unlike us) in regarding as invariable and independent of a culture's changing systems of manufacture and variables of religious belief. It would indeed be unfortunate if the contemporary enthusiasm for the history of technology were to obscure the more infantile scenes played out in the drama of figuration: the whole stratum of religiosity which lies dormant, preserved, packed away, and concentrated beneath all our games and fireworks, that underworld of sedimented affective responses and confused values wherein we can always read the struggle of the quick to ward off death, forestall emptiness, and hold back the fleeting of time.* How could we forget

---

*In Chapter 1 of *Vie et mort de l'image* Debray argues that the primordial function of the archaic *eidôlon* (which had the sense of phantom or spirit before coming to mean an image or portrait) was to replace the dead on earth. The practice can be traced back to the Greek *kolossos* and *kouros*, effigies of the deceased, and to the funerary sarcaphogi of the Egyptians. [Trs.]

such a foundation, when the visible image (and especially the index, a kind of "childhood of the sign") practices "the return upstream" dear to René Char. It causes the viewer to dig back to that "primal processing" of the psychic mechanism (condensation, figuration-as-displacement) by exhibiting its darker side of hunting ritual and necromancy. The deeds of figuration part company with the deeds of discourse further by compelling us to pick up both ends of the narrative chain of its story, the lab and the painted cave, hi-tech and the primitive forest. A fractal or virtual image amounts to a meta-picture; a Christ or Mary figure from the Auvergne, seated on the throne and hieratically treated, or a Byzantine *theothokos*, can be called proto-"artworks"; and it is in the straits between them that mediological history evolves from the banks of one age to the other. There would be a danger in truly choosing either the futurism of digitized imagery or the archaism of Cycladean idols, because the archaic—even more in the case of the imagistic than the political—turns out to be not what is behind but rather underneath.

That is why we have begun the study by examining acts of looking that one might call *déshabillés* (by that I mean unassisted by apparatuses of looking)—without microscope, telescope or computer. This primitive or rather primordial gaze took the form of fright at ghosts, at doubles, at all the corporeally refined yet nevertheless identifiable beings into which a dead person had passed. A pragmatic history of looking would remain unduly speculative indeed were it to overlook this initial sacred function of idols which endured for a considerable period. During this time the soul was a great force and thus the image took on what was virtually the same power. Image-makers at first created representations of the dead and the absent to hold them fast, otherwise their *anima* would begin to float everywhere, harrying people and destabilizing the fixed order of things. We the viewers would not be haunted by visible formations if the idol-image had not, itself, been for so long inhabited by, been the haunt of, the spirit. Both miraculous and maleficent, it attracted and instilled fear, fascinated and terrified, because it was not after all a vulgar copy, a false appearance, but a standing in place of: a magic ambivalence. The first photographic portraits revived the effect it must have had, toward 1860, when they were felt to be as magnetic as they were frightening ("we believed them capable of seeing *us!*"). The dead subsisted in the image that stood for them—and by "image" here is meant the three-dimensional idol, a stele or some other sign set in the ground, but also the oneiric vision, Patroclus appearing to Achilles in a dream, the animated double of an animate body. Before it became appearance, the idol was an apparition brandished as a counter to *disparition*, to disappearance: a power of evocation in the hands of the survivors. This enabling substitution occasioned a free circulation of the living among the dead by abolishing the lines of demarcation between them, not in order to turn the former into mourners but to revitalize the latter. We can still see the vitalism, exuberance and gaiety in the tomb art of traditional societies like Haiti. Representational forms have for a long time served to bring something of the invisible world into the visible. The beginnings of the Christian era show this direct relation between the cult of the dead and of carved images in the phenomenon of saints' relics. It is found as well in the cult of sacred remnants from the true Cross (indexical relics tied to geographical location), or the likenesses of the crucifix (analogical, portable and universal). The statuary-reliquary of the Holy Virgin or saint is an object of worship because it contains the corporeal remains that give off their radiance through it, transferring the sacredness of the missing body to its preserved and "restored" receptacle-image. There are today chemical or electronic images we still unconsciously look at as "relics," and our profane picturings and iconography are perhaps the last remainder of a relic.

The desacralization of images in the videosphere, thanks to their endless tide whose pull is industrial and commercial, relegates this bygone regime of belief to the margins. It is a process analogous to the desacralization of the text through printing. Yet how could thousands of years of thaumaturgic, preventive, devotional, magical practices not have left something of their trace in the unconsciousness of the modern eye? The magical gaze for which divine and human make their rounds as part of the same cosmic life-force is no longer our own; then again, it is not something subject to the calculations of profit and loss. The return of the dead is far from moribund. For evidence see the spellbinding power still exerted by the shroud of Turin over contemporary visionaries (scientists included) even after its carbon-dating and the recognition of its fraudulence by its custodian the archbishop of Turin in 1988. See Barthes' late fascination with the photograph's funereal radiance, its *spectrum* (from *specere*, "to look") and *punctum* (from *pungere*, "to sting or prick"), its posthumous poignancy.* Pictorial elaborations of the resurrection's mournful colors, and the image itself *as* a resurrection, are endless.

The passage from magic to science, one should remember, is not a one-way street. Far from killing the aura Benjamin spoke of, the photograph perhaps even revived it (for a while). Witness the discoverer of X-rays, the German physicist Wilhelm Roentgen, who asserted an affinity between his invisible light and a mysterious "vibration of the ether" (1895), and found sustenance in spiritualism. Witness the negative taken of the Turin shroud (Secundo Pia, 1898), which seemed to objectify and typify its mystique as miracle. Claudel remarked of it, "It's a tracing, a divine image, whose guarantee of authenticity stands or falls only with itself. More than a depiction, it is a presence!" (*La Photographie du Christ*, 1936). The holy shroud: the first "photograph" (of the Christian era: there had been others produced in this form before). Photography: the poor man's holy shroud. Or perhaps his "Veronica" [an imprint left on cloth, as on the handkerchief preserved at Rome supposedly surviving from Saint Veronica's gesture of wiping the suffering Christ's face as she followed him up Calvary], a profanated Veronica made multiple, innumerable and banal. The "true icon," the "victorious," sits in state on our dressers and mantles in the form of grandfather's photograph. The least yellowed print "unmade by the hand of man" brings back the ancient flutter here in the heart of the family of that white sheet of the origin, that *mandylion* applied by Veronica on the Holy Face at the sixth station of the Cross, whereupon Christ's visage left its imprint—actually deposited

---

*See Roland Barthes, *Camera Lucida: Reflections on Photography*, tr. Richard Howard (New York: Hill and Wang, 1981). The relevant pages in the original can be found in Roland Barthes, *La Chambre claire: note sur la photographie* (Paris: Gallimard, 1980), pp. 22–3 and 69. [Trs.]

its lines rather than copying them. He was felt to be there not by resemblance but substance, flesh and blood. Let us now consider at random the printing of a picture: it is no longer a linen-cloth but a piece of paper. But it carries on its surface the *imprint* of a body, a spiritual body materially preserved among us, a physical double spiritually present in our midst. The indexical image, somewhere between ectoplasm and emanation, reawakens the idolatrous gaze. And photography proves to be a psychography: in its way it brings back Ulysses in the underworld, pouring out libations of wine to the shades.

The question why over the course of human history people have produced sculptures and pictures rather than nothing, admits then (and has for along time) of a plausible explanation: because human beings are the only animals that know they are mortal. If we want to get to the heart of the matter this would be the anthropological answer. It is also the film critic's who would evoke (as André Bazin does in his *Ontologie de l'image photographique*) "the mummy complex," that is, statues and paintings and movies as a latter-day surrogate mummification invented to embalm time and save the being of things by fixing their appearance. (As it was said of Louis XIV that "instead of having himself embalmed he is satisfied to have his portrait painted by Lebrun.") We can verify this general or generic answer in texts or on the basis of traces that are still available. But to the properly historical question, which is just as enigmatic, "Why were representational forms produced in the West after 325 A.D., the year of Constantine's conversion?" for an answer we can only look to theology.

Such a momentous development was not a foregone conclusion—because monotheism, with its origins in scripture, is of its nature at the very most "an-iconic" (indifferent to an ontology or metaphysics of the visible), if not iconoclastic. It was the visibility in the sense of *viewability* of the Son of God, elevated into dogma with the Church's adoption of the Incarnation, that legitimated human access to the spiritual through the perceptible. This legitimation was not without its attendant evils: from the acts of Byzantine emperors to the Calvinists of Geneva, including the Waldovian heresy of twelfth century France (named after its founder Peter Waldo) opposed to any doctrines not literally contained in the Bible, as well as the Hussites, there was no shortage of iconoclasts, and the battle was fierce. The authorized access to the Word through the image of God's Image had its corollary in the access to God through Christ. And this is an astonishing answer all the same, in that it does not seem to break in a radical way with the animistic and polytheistic past. The representational image as a bridge or relay between a nature and a supernature—what is this if not an idol? Theologians spent several centuries trying to dispel the ambiguity. But whatever its internal contradictions, the genius or "ingenium" of the Christian religion did function as the genetic code of a civilization. This is what we had in mind in asserting that Hollywood was born in Byzantium (or rather at Nicea at the time of its Seventh Council regulating image worship in 787). Was Reason "the Greek miracle"? If so let us say that the manufacture of images was the marvel of Christendom. The West was "programmed" by incarnation, and thus representation.

From this there resulted a singular formal dynamism unlike anything before, since the icon in the Christian East remained static (a *theotokos* of the fifteenth century is no different formally from its homologous ancestor from the tenth century). Western religious representation in the medieval age, as Le Goff, Schmitt and others have shown, developed the freedom to humanize the celestial powers (Christ and the Holy Virgin) and divinize terrestrial ones (transforming the king into his effigy)—to the point of liberating an autonomous space that came to be occupied by a distinct worldly power and its accompaniment, a secular art. The configuration of sight in the medieval period, however, has not appeared to us qualitatively different from the pagan vision, and the notion we put forth of the idol (in a non-polemical sense) can believably bring together these two sides of the hill whose apex marks the before from the after of the life of Christ. There are indeed three conditions by which we can recognize the "idol": 1) the "transitive" value of the visible image, painted or sculpted, as a simple relay point toward the unseen, serving to render it visible; 2) the act of beholding it, which is neither aesthetically contemplative nor individual but welded to a full and collective participation, from within the space of worship or liturgical procession; and 3) its manufacture, arising not from a singled out and highly valued classification of individual creators (the cathedrals were decorated simply by "workers," and the carver of African fetishes can be at the same time a basket-maker, a shepherd or a medicine man).

The centering of this communitarian gaze in a new subjectivity, as a corollary of the scientific objectification of nature, opened the way in Europe to the appearance of "art" and the "artist" in the age of printing. Its advent is made possible by its slow decoupling from ecclesiastical direction and the theological world order (God as the sole creator). Several transitions occur over this period (the Trecento in Italy, later elsewhere): from the *idol* to the *work*, from the object of worship to that of delectation, from artisan to artist, presence to representation, the supernatural to nature, the personified image to the image as thing. During this time are born landscape, the self-portrait, the history of art and the legend of the artist as biographical personality. All these episodes are taken up in due course in our study.

The Renaissance, in brief, multiplies works of visual imagination but weakens the powers of visual form and the object as a medium of divinity. The historical succession of their functions—to ensure survival, then pleasure, and last, information—exhibits a downturn in the energetic or charismatic output of the objects of the Western eye. From the idol—a form that looks at or through me from on high—to the "visual"—a form constructed by me which can only refer my look to other images, our gaze has been formed and informed by theology, aesthetics, and then electronics. The image on which it has fixed its attention seems to lose its reserves of "cash in hand" and transmit less and less energy.

This trajectory of the structures of visibility, spiraling so manifestly downward, raises the question whether an anthropology of the Western eye would appropriately come under what Lévi-Strauss called a generalized "entropology." Or to put it more simply, have I given in to a *passéiste* vision of things, a reactive aesthetics, and the critical temptation of proffering the nth denunciatory diagnosis of a mechanistic decline? What seems readily granted is that a metamorphosing mediation of the supernatural (by the idol), of nature (by art), and of oneself (the paradigm of advertising) translates a certain enfeeblement of the symbols produced. On reflection I wonder if by perhaps over-valuing an aesthetic of disappearance (through the myths of the holy shroud or the ghostliness of photography), one ends up indeed seeing in today's automatized imagery (a reproducible sequence of impersonal operations) nothing more than a disap-pearance of the Aesthetic. This would be an unfair way of looking at things, or a reactive one (there are, after all, *different* aesthetics). In starker terms, I asked myself whether I had not unconsciously taken up what François Guéry would call the reactionary critique of industrial values. I think not, finally: even if the magical dynamism of the look in its idol phase marks the very highest degree of visual efficacy, nothing still leads inex-orably to the conclusion that we are dealing with some "state of nature" to be essentialized as a universal standard or archetype. It seems to me that it is a question of man's relation with artifacts from the very beginning, even in the case of the medieval *ymagiers*. There is therefore no degeneration of the natural into the artificial, of the true into the false, and even less so of the refined into the vulgar.[*]

As a practice, through the relative lightening of its material base and techniques, and the deterritorialization of its networks of production and consumption, the visual image has rather taken an ascensional direction in modern times—from a (low-technological) unwieldiness toward a (high-tech) fleetness, from a folkloric localism toward a disembodied globality. I hope then not to have yielded uncritically to a much too negative concep-tion of the sterile "repeatability" of cultural forms—Benjamin's "mechanical reproduction"—which would binarize copy and original, or mechanistic and vital. But since I had resolved to

---

[*]Debray's argument here about the inappropriateness of distinctions between natural and artificial or cultural in discussing human beings' relation to their visible artifacts is paralleled by the thesis in anthropology that technology as well has been a part of their development "from the beginning." A classic statement of this position was made by Sherwood Washburn in "Tools and Human Evolution," *Scientific American* 203, no. 3 (September 1960), pp. 63–75. For elaborations on it, see Bruce Mazlish, *The Fourth Discontinuity: The Co-Evolution of Humans and Machines* (New Haven: Yale University Press, 1993) and André Leroi-Gourhan, *Gesture and Speech*, tr. Anna Bostock Berger (Cambridge: MIT Press, 1993). [Trs.]

keep the balance equal between the questions of technology and belief, I freely admit to having surrendered nothing, conversely, to the "optimistic positivism" (Alain Gras' phrase) that would see in each technological leap of visual production an unambiguous advance of progress with no consideration given to what it leaves behind. Infography and cyberspace do not as a matter of fact seem to me something over which one should uncritically go into raptures.

Evoking the idea of a history of visual forms that have become "desacralized" is not in any case to announce the demise of all the ancient credulities, and still less to obsess about coming back to a lost origin of ocular and religious naivete (even if any man-made image beheld by the eye re-stages endlessly the viewer's curiosity about its origination). My intention is to make us rethink the reworking and displacement that "perceptual faith" has undergone, and, awaiting evidence to the contrary, to not second all those who in our day believe they no longer believe in anything. We find ourselves at present in the era of "visual" credulity, that is, when representations of the world are no longer carried by a lived experience of it. Under such conditions, idolatry has made something of a comeback. I daresay it is, however, a rather perverted or devalued, unstable and melancholically perishable idolatry (with one idol ceaselessly giving way to the next, like TV programs). An age of audiovisuality reactivates in its own way the immemorial urgency to believe, and just as often disappoints it. Its manner of enticing without satisfying, or of garnering credibility without truly giving anything to credit, will perhaps one day come to seem a fleeting historical moment among others—certainly not the least plausible but not the most emancipated either—of the beliefs we invest or embody in the things we see.

This is all that this brief outline of a history of the Western eye was meant to suggest. Localized in those latitudes of the human look, it makes its contribution to what one day could be called a historical anthropology of Western beliefs.

APPENDICES

Mediological Tables

Excerpt from *Cours de médiologie générale*

	WRITING (LOGOSPHERE)	PRINTED TEXT (GRAPHOSPHERE)	AUDIOVISUAL (VIDEOSPHERE)
STRATEGIC MILIEU (PROJECTED POWER)	THE EARTH	THE SEA	SPACE
GROUP IDEAL (AND POLITICS)	THE ONE (City, Empire, Kingdom) absolutism	EVERYONE (Nation, People, State) nationalism, totalitarianism	EACH ONE (population, society, world) individualism and anomie
SHAPE OF TIME (AND ITS VECTOR)	CIRCLE (Eternal repetition) Archeocentric	LIGNE (history, Progress) FUTUROCENTRIC	POINT (news, event) EGOCENTRIC: cult of the present
CANONICAL PHASE OF LIFESPAN	THE ELDER	THE ADULT	THE YOUNG PERSON
PARADIGMATIC ATTRACTION	MYTHOS (mysteries, dogmas, epics)	LOGOS (utopias, systems, programs)	IMAGO (emotions and fantasms)
SYMBOLIC ORGANON	RELIGIONS (theology)	SYSTEMS (ideologies)	MODELS (iconology)
SPIRITUAL CLASS (CONTROLS SOCIAL SACRED)	CHURCH (prophets, clerics) Sacrosanct: DOGMA	INTELLIGENTSIA secular (professors, doctors) Sacrosanct: KNOWLEDGE	MEDIAS (broadcasters and producers) Sacrosanct: INFORMATION
REFERENCE OF LEGITIMACY	THE DIVINE (we must, it is sacred)	THE IDEAL (we must, it is true)	THE PERFORMER (we must, for it works)
MOTIVATOR OF OBEDIENCE	FAITH (fanaticism)	LAW (dogmatism)	OPINION (relativism)
REGULAR MEANS OF INFLUENCE	PREACHING	PUBLICATION	VISIBILITY
CONTROL OF INFORMATION	ECCLESIASTICAL, DIRECT (over utterers)	POLITICAL, INDIRECT (over means of sending)	ECONOMIC, INDIRECT (over messages)
STATUS OF INDIVIDUAL	SUBJECT (to command)	CITIZEN (to convince)	CONSUMER (to seduce)
MYTH OF IDENTIFICATION	THE SAINT	THE HERO	THE STAR
MOTTO OF PERSONAL AUTHORITY	"GOD TOLD IT TO ME" (true like words from the Gospel)	"I READ IT IN A BOOK" (true like a printed word)	"I SAW IT ON TV" (true like a live broadcast)
REGIME OF SYMBOLIC AUTHORITY	THE INVISIBLE (Origin) or the unverifiable	THE READABLE (Foundation) or true logic	THE VISIBLE (Event) or the plausible
UNIT OF SOCIAL DIRECTION	THE SYMBOLIC ONE: the King (dynastic principle)	THE THEORETICAL ONE: the Head (ideological principle)	THE ARITHMETICAL ONE: the Leader (statistical principle, poles, rating, audience)
CENTER OF SUBJECTIVE GRAVITY	THE SOUL (Anima)	CONSCIOUSNESS (Animus)	THE BODY (Sensorium)

Excerpt from *A History of the Western Eye*

ATTRIBUTES OF THE IMAGE	IN THE LOGOSPHERE **(after writing)** REGIME OF THE IDOL	IN THE GRAPHOSPHERE **(after printing)** REGIME OF ART	IN THE VIDEOSPHERE **(after the audiovisual)** REGIME OF THE VISUAL
PRINCIPLE OF ITS EFFICACY (OR RELATION TO BEING)	PRESENCE (transcendent) The image sees	REPRESENTATION (illusory) The image is seen	SIMULATION (numerical) The image is viewed
MODE OF EXISTENCE	LIVING The image is a being	PHYSICAL The image is a thing	VIRTUAL The image is perceived
CRUCIAL REFERENT (SOURCE OF AUTHORITY)	THE SUPERNATURAL (God)	THE REAL (Nature)	THE PERFORMER (The Machine)
SOURCE OF LIGHT	SPIRITUAL (from within)	SOLAR (from without)	ELECTRIC (from within)
PURPOSE AND EXPECTATION	PROTECTION (& salvation) The image captures	DELECTATION (& prestige) The image captivates	INFORMATION (& game-playing) The image is captured
HISTORICAL CONTEXT	From MAGICAL to RELIGIOUS (Cyclical Time)	From the RELIGIOUS to the HISTORICAL (Linear Time)	From the HISTORICAL to the TECHNICAL (Punctual Time)
DEONTOLOGY	EXTERNAL (theological & political organization)	INTERNAL (autonomous administration)	AMBIENT (Techno-economic management)
IDEAL & NORM OF WORK	"I CELEBRATE" (a force) Modeled on Scripture (Canon)	"I CREATE" (a work) Modeled on antiquity (Model)	"I PRODUCE" (an event) Modeled on the Ego (Fashion)
TEMPORAL HORIZON (& MEDIUM)	ETERNITY (repetition) Hardness (stone, wood)	IMMORTALITY (tradition) Softness (canvas)	THE PRESENT (innovation) Immateriality (screen)
MODE OF ATTRIBUTION	COLLECTIVE=ANONYMOUS (from sorcerer to artisan)	INDIVIDUAL=SIGNATURE (from artist to genius)	SPECTACULAR=LABEL, LOGO BRAND NAME (from entrepreneur to enterprise)
ORGANIZATION OF LABOR	From CLERISY to GUILD	From ACADEMY to SCHOOL	From NETWORK to PROFESSION
OBJECT OF WORSHIP	THE SAINT (I protect you)	BEAUTY (I am pleasing)	NOVELTY (I surprise you)
GOVERNMENTAL STRUCTURE	1) CURIAL=The Emperor 2) ECCLESIASTICAL= Monasteries & Cathedrals 3) SEIGNORIAL= The Palace	1) MONARCHICAL=The Academy (1500-1750) 2) BOURGEOISIE=Salon + Criticism + Gallery (to 1968)	MEDIA/MUSEUM/MARKET (for plastic arts) PUBLICITY (audiovisual)
CONTINENT OF ORIGIN & CITY OF TRANSMISSION	ASIA-BYZANTIUM (between antiquity and Christianity)	EUROPE-FLORENCE (between Christianity and modernity)	AMERICA-NEW YORK (between modern and postmodern)
MODE OF ACCUMULATION	PUBLIC: The treasury	INDIVIDUAL: The collection	PRIVATE/PUBLIC: Reproduction
AURA	CHARISMATIC (anima)	PATHETIC (animus)	LUDIC (animation)
PATHOLOGICAL TENDENCY	PARANOIA	OBSESSION	SCHIZOPHRENIA
AIM OF THE GAZE	ACROSS THE IMAGE Clairvoyance conveys	MORE THAN THE IMAGE Vision contemplates	ONLY THE IMAGE Viewing controls
MUTUAL RELATIONS	INTOLERANCE (Religious)	RIVALRY (Personal)	COMPETITION (Economic)

Excerpt from *L'État séducteur*

	LOGOSPHERE	GRAPHOSPHERE		VIDEOSPHERE
IDEAL TYPE	FEUDAL MONARCHY (PRE-RENAISSANCE)	ABSOLUTE MONARCHY (1650-1789)	REPUBLIC (1900)	DEMOCRACY (2000)
THE SYMBOLIC ONE FUNCTIONS AS . . .	MAGICIAN KING (Age of miracles)	STAGECRAFTING KING (Age of marvels)	MECHANICAL "KING" (Age of motors)	TECHNOLOGIC "KING" (Age of montage)
STATUS OF THE GOVERNED	THE FAITHFUL (SUPRAPOLITICAL) assembly: the Church	THE SUBJECT (METAPOLITICS) assembly: the Kingdom	THE CITIZEN (POLITICS) assembly: the Nation	TV VIEWER (INFRA-POLITICS) assembly: the Market
NATURE OF STATE IMAGERY	HERALDIC (arms, emblems, mottos) shield with fleur-de-lis	ICONOGRAPHIC (gallery of faces) the King's portrait	ALLEGORICAL (personification of ideas) Marianne	"SIGNAL-ETICAL" (logos, name tags, slogan) Visual
PRESTIGE OF LEADER	SACREDNESS (direct link with Christ: sacred *king*)	MAJESTY (indirect link, king *mediates* sacred)	GLORY (indirect link with Reason and Progress)	AURA (direct link with population)
IDEAL SITE OF EXALTATION	ALTAR (Church)	THE SCENE (theater)	LECTURER'S PLATFORM (school)	SCREEN (TV)
RITUAL OF PRESENTATION	LITURGY (on one's knees)	THE CEREMONIAL (to amaze)	DISCOURSE (to convince)	THE TV SHOW (to seduce)
NATURE OF FESTIVITIES	RELIGIOUS (processions, canticles)	ARISTOCRATIC OR MYTHOLOGICAL (court festival: opera, ball, concert)	UTOPIAN OR COMMEMORATIVE (Festival of Reason, July 14)	MEDIATIC OR RECREATIVE (festival of music)
SOVEREIGN'S SIGN-MAKING	I INTERPRET (such is God's will)	I POINT TO (such is my wish)	I EXPLAIN (such is the truth)	I GIVE NEWS (such is reality)
SYMBOLIC OFFER	YOU HAVE RIGHT TO TOUCH (scrofula)	YOU HAVE RIGHT TO LOOK AT (at court)	YOU HAVE RIGHT TO LEARN (school)	YOU HAVE RIGHT TO REPLY (the poll)
TRANSFIGURATION BY THE IMAGE	RELIGIOUS (S/he's a saint!)	HEROIC (He's an Apollo!)	PEDAGOGICAL (He's a Maestro!)	PUBLICITARIAN (S/he's a star!)
MEANS OF MAKING AUTHORITY BE CEDED	BY DEVOTION	BY BEDAZZLING	BY INDOCTRINATION	BY MANIPULATION
PHYSICAL CARRYING OF SIGN	HORSE/MAN Speed: horse	ROAD/MAN Speed: horse, boat	RAIL/WIRE Speed: steam, electricity	ELECTRON/SATELLITE Speed: light
APOTHEOSIS: WHERE GO THE REMAINS OF THE FAMOUS?	IN THE CHURCH (Eschatological pantheon)	IN THE PALACE (Monarchical pantheon)	IN MUSEUM, MAYORALITY, SQUARE (Civic pantheon)	ON THE SCREEN (Audiovisual pantheon)
BODILY ATTITUDE OF THE HONORED DEAD	RECUMBENT EFFIGY (praying dead)	EQUESTRIAL STATUE (funeral oration)	STANDING FIGURE (written panegyric)	THE POSTER (necrology)
SPECTACLE'S USE	TO ADORE	TO ENCHANT	TO ILLUSTRATE	TO ENTERTAIN
BEST-SELLER TITLE	POWER & IDOL	POWER & GOD	POWER & IDEAL	POWER & LIFE
MYSTIQUE OF REIGNING "I"	I AM THE CHRIST Emblem: phoenix (13th century)	*L'ETAT, C'EST MOI* Emblem: the Sun (17th century)	I AM THE NATION Emblem: the rooster (19th c.)	I AM THE MAJORITY Emblem: nothing
PUBLIC OPINION	(not applicable)	THE PEOPLE'S WORD (rumor, cry, echo, murmur or . . .)	THE PUBLICATION OF OPINION (newspapers, books, pamphlets)	THE RESPONSE TO A SPECIALIZED SURVEY (polls)
ITS SUBJECT	—	THE POPULACE (opinion disregarded)	THE PUBLIC OR LEARNED THINKERS (opinion feared)	THE INDIVIDUAL (opinion quantified)
MANIFESTS . . .	—	THE UNREASON of individuals	Universal REASON	Individual FREEDOM
CONTROL BY . . .	—	CHURCH/ACADEMIES	SCHOOL/ INSTITUTIONS	COMMUNICATION/ CORPORATIONS

Word vs. Letter

INSTITUTIONS AND POWERS OF THE WORD	INSTITUTIONS AND POWERS OF THE LETTER
ORAL TRADITION	WRITTEN TRADITION
RELEVANCIES OF AUTHORITY (sphere of belief)	RELEVANCIES OF TRUTH (sphere of knowledge)
STATEMENT OF FACT: values of affect	STATEMENT OF RIGHT: values of ideas
THOUGHT IN SITUATION (the voice connects)	DECONTEXTUALIZED THOUGHT (written text displaces)
OVERPRESENCE OF THE PRESENT	OVERPRESENCE PAST/FUTURE
EMPHATIC AND PARTICIPATORY COMMUNICATION (force of context)	ANALYTICAL AND CUMULATIVE COMMUNICATION (force of the "co-text")
ADDITIVE LOGIC (juxtaposing)	SUBORDINATIVE LOGIC (make sequential)
AGGREGATIVE SYNTHESIS (redundance)	DISCRIMINATIVE ANALYSIS (distance)
SUGGESTIVE POWER OF HEARING (social immersion)	SEPARATING POWER OF THE EYE (critical distancing)
TRADITIONALIST FACILITY (difficult to criticize one's public in real time)	DOGMATIC FACILITY (ease with which a public can be sado-masochized at a distance)
VALUES OF COMPLICITY AND IMPATIENCE (phatic)	VALUES OF PATIENCE AND COHERENCE (optical)
PERSONALIZATION OF SOCIAL LINK	APTITUDE FOR IMPERSONAL LIFE
POLEMICAL HABITUS *ad hominem* (but open mind)	LOGICAL HABITUS IN A UNIVERSAL MODE (but closed-mindedness)
KNOWING IS THROUGH THE ACT: primacy of praxis	KNOWLEDGE IS STORED: primacy of the opus
AUTHORITY OF AUTHORS WITHOUT WORK "LISTEN TO THE DIFFERENCE"	AUTHORITY OF WORKS WITHOUT AUTHOR "SEE THE DIFFERENCE"

Glossary

On the one hand, care must be taken not to fall into the pretences of formalism: one does not create a useful concept just by coining a neologism. On the other, a commitment must be made to being precise: no refutability nor even discussion are possible without a definition of terms. The semantic confusion of numerous ongoing debates about "communication" leads to the conclusion that, of the two, a rudimentary lexicon will always prove a less grievous flaw than a charming rhetorical cloud. All things considered, the social sciences require this basic courtesy.

circuit, short: drop in status of the class of mediators operating within a demoted earlier medium, whose efficiency of profit-making has been weakened by a new medium.

cultural crisis: initial effect of overlapping two or several competing memory technologies.

effect, jogging: renewal of the old by the new. Complement and correction of the ratchet effect (*q.v.*, below) (motorists who walk less run more).

effect, ratchet (*passim*): irreversibility of technological progress. Firearm users do not turn back to the crossbow after the harquebus; nor do travellers revert to the stagecoach after the railroad.

effect, stagecoach (Jacques Perriault's term): the new begins by imitating the old. The design of the first railroad cars looked like the horse-drawn coach. The first incunabula were made to look like manuscripts; the first photographs, like oil paintings; the first films, like plays in the theater; the first television set, like a radio receiver that broadcast images; etc.

graphosphere: period initiated by the technology of printing; transmission chiefly by books of knowledge and myths.

high-, low-intelligentsia: hierarchy in which producers of symbols function, determined by their access or non-access to the central means of transmission.

ideologies, history of: supplement of the history of technologies (of association and transmission).

logosphere: period initiated by the technology of writing; mainly oral transmission or rare sacred texts.

mediabolic, a (organ): the particular miracle-tool of a mediasphere, organizer of time and space, receptacle of ambivalences. E.g., the human voice, the book, the television, the computer.

mediasphere: megasystem of transmission (and of transportation). We can divide historical times into three principal periods (*logo-, grapho-,* and *videosphere*).

mediatheme: elementary unit of social mythologies mobilized and legitimized by a technology of transmission ("God" is a logotheme; "humankind," a graphotheme; the "Humanitarian," a videotheme).

mediocracy: elite holding the means of production of mass opinion. More widely, state of society in which the intermediaries of broadcasting and dissemination predominate (*Teachers, Writers, Celebrities*, 1979).

mediorhythm: average time needed for a symbolic corpus to spread or be distributed in the mediasphere (the logosphere's unit of calculation is centuries and decades; the graphosphere's is years; the videosphere's, days).

mediospace: relation of a given surface area to a speed for covering it, the territorial variable of the mediasphere ("the French hexagon whose sides are but an hour away").

medium: system of material base and procedures of memory storage, articulated against a network that distributes signals or traces.

metatext: the entire set of peripheral directions pertaining to the legitimate use of a text.

mneumosphere: medium and setting of a *purely* oral transmission preceding the invention of alphabets—from father to son, teacher to disciple, etc.

nostalgia: the first phase of mediological consciousness. The discovery of a clear deviation from the old norm grasps the new order as a disordering. More deeply: an intuition of the entropy of systems.

patrimony, cultural: store of traces accessible in a given framework (local, regional, national, human).

performance, index of: susceptibleness to being transmitted, proper to a given regime of utterance or statement in a given mediasphere (e.g., critical rationality has a socially weak index in the logosphere, a higher "reading" in the graphosphere, and is minimal in the videosphere).

spectacle: method of theatrical representation based on a double spatio-temporal separation—between a spectator and a scene, between an actor and an action. In a word, based on the "semiotic break" representation/represented. E.g., theater and film are spectacles, not a televisual live broadcasting.

"society of the spectacle" (Guy Debord): a technological archaism. The videosphere, which tends to abolish it, makes its loss missed.

supporting material base: surface on which traces are inscribed.

thought (doctrine, religion, discipline): process of organizing a sequence of transmission. Branch of logistics (supply, transportation, accommodation).

trace: any setting down of a record or recording. The minimal object of archiving.

videosphere: period that begins with the advent of audiovisual technology; a transmission of data, models and narratives mainly by viewing them on screen.

Select Bibliography

The works listed here are only those more recent writings of Debray on mediological subjects. Translations in English given if available.

Cours de médiologie générale (Paris: Gallimard, 1991).

Critique de la raison politique ou l'inconscient religieux (Paris: Gallimard, 1981). Translated by David Macey under the title Critique of Political Reason (London: Verso, 1983).

L'État séducteur: les révolutions médiologiques du pouvoir (Paris: Gallimard, 1993).

L'Oeil naïf (Paris: Éditions du Seuil, 1994).

Le Pouvoir intellectuel en France (Paris: Gallimard, 1979). Translated by David Macey under the title Teachers, Writers, Celebrities (London: Verso, 1981).

"A propos du spectacle. Réponse à un jeune chercheur" [essay on Guy Debord] and "Chemin faisant," in Le Débat, no. 85 (May–August 1995), pp. 3–15 and 53–61. [Issue includes articles on Mediology by Roger Chartier, Dany-Robert Dufour, Roger Laufer, Jean-Louis Missika, Bernard Stiegler.]

Le Scribe: Génèse du politique (Paris: Gallimard, 1980).

Vie et mort de l'image: une histoire du regard en Occident (Paris: Gallimard, 1992).Translation, A History of the Western Eye, forthcoming.

Select articles, excerpts, and interviews in English:

"The Book as Symbolic Object" [On Sartre's *Les Mots*]. Essay appearing in forthcoming anthology of papers presented at the San Marino conference on the Book (Spring 1994), sponsored by the Centro di Studi Semiotici e Cognitivi, University of Bologna. Edited by Geoffrey Nunberg (University of California Press).

"The Image vs. Language," *Common Knowledge,* vol. 4, no. 2 (Fall 1995). Originally published as "La Transmission symbolique," Chapter II in Debray, *Vie et mort de l'image*, pp. 43–73.

"The Myth of Art," *ViceVersa* 49 (July/September 1995), pp. 30–34. Originally published as "La spirale sans fin de l'histoire" and "Une religion désespérée," Chapters V and IX (from which excerpted pages taken), Debray, *Vie et mort de l'image*, pp. 155–9 and 261–5.

"Revolution in the Revolution" (interview with Andrew Joscelyne), in *Wired* 3.01 (January 1995), pp. 116 and 161–2.

"The Small Screen Favors Caesar" (interview), in *NPQ*, vol. 11, no. 4 (Fall 1994), pp. 43–4.

"The Three Ages of Looking," in *Critical Inquiry* 21 (Spring 1995), pp. 529–55. Originally published as "Les trois âges du regard," Chapter VIII in Debray, *Vie et mort de l'image*, pp. 219–54.

"Universal Art: The Desperate Religion," in *NPQ*, vol. 9, no. 2 (Spring 1992), pp. 35–41.